Effective Marketing for Lawyers

Effective Marketing for Lawyers

Christine S. Filip, Esq.

New York State Bar Association

Written & Edited by
Christine S. Filip, Esq.

Contributing Authors:
Kathleen Waits, Esq.
Stephen P. Gallagher
J. Richardson Lippert, II, Esq.
Russell Pearce, Esq.
Bruce Green, Esq.

Published jointly by the Special Committee on
Solo and Small Firm Practitioners, the Department of Law Office
Economics and Management and the Continuing Legal Education
Department of the New York State Bar Association

Library of Congress Catalog Card Number: 95-11790
ISBN: 0-942954-78-5

Cover Design by The Type & Design Center, Inc.
Cover Photo: © Paul Epley/Picturesque, 1995

Foreword

MARKETING PROFESSIONAL SERVICES isn't a subject that's taught in law schools, which is why the New York State Bar Association published this book. Since the introduction of lawyer advertising, competition for new business has become increasingly fierce in the profession, and with that competition has come a need for lawyers to market themselves in a way that's sophisticated, ethical and effective. This book tells you how.

You will learn which of three types of clients is the most profitable for you to retain: Level One clients are profitable, pay on time, and bring you work; Level Two clients are marginally profitable but are susceptible to expansion or are fertile referral sources; Level Three clients are not profitable, bring you the wrong type of work, and demand too much. Do you know how to increase your Level Ones (which are 20 percent of your client base but generate 80 percent of your fees) and avoid Level Threes? This book tells you how.

By using the sample checklists and forms, this book explains how to increase your client base, recognize new opportunities for delivering legal services, and develop your practice. If you are a woman or minority lawyer, you will be particularly interested in the discussion of rainmaking and ways to overcome the peculiar difficulties you may face in developing your business. Solo and small-firm practitioners will also find "Effective Marketing for Lawyers" to be a valuable reference.

We know that in order for you to achieve and maintain success in today's competitive environment, you must have a strategic marketing game plan. This book gives you that competitive edge.

G. Robert Witmer, Jr.
Past President
New York State Bar Association

Introduction

I HAVE THIS one particular dream a couple of times a year. I wake up in the thin light of dawn in a cold sweat thinking that I have slept through the start of the bar exam. This is a 14-year-old dream, and when I fully wake up, I'm relieved. Yet, at the same instant of relief, some nagging questions persist — Was it worth it? What did law school prepare me for, really?

Certainly not for marketing. My actual work life prepared me for that as I slogged through night school as a sales, marketing, and general manager. But for many of my colleagues, no program or institution has adequately prepared them for managing the business development process in their practices. Worse still, much of the marketing advice available advises low payback, high-expense tactics which fuel the argument that marketing is unprofessional, if not unethical.

Without debating the issue of whether marketing is a professional activity, beyond the comment that marketing, per se, merely describes a human communication and decision-making process that began with the advent of enterprise, I view the question of professionalism as moot. It merely holds up the economic learning curve to undeserved scrutiny and begs the wrong question.

I believe that the more valid question is, *What* types of marketing strategies best serve the ethical and professional interests of both client and lawyer? I believe they are *not* competing interests. Professional business strategies ought to embellish, not erode, the ideal of legal professionalism and the dream of establishing a worthy practice that serves up high-quality client services.

"Professional" and "business" put together is not an oxymoron, but a description, like "S corp" or "limited liability company." "Professional" and "business" do, however, connote some economic realities worthy of highlighting up front. There's little need to recount the shifting competitive forces that have changed the landscape for practicing law; we all know them well. That the practice of law is subject to the evolution of the marketplace is not necessarily an unprofessional nor an unethical proposition. It merely exists as a fact. How we respond as a profession is critical.

That marketing, per se, should be, and is, germane to the practice of law bespeaks the economic reality of the profession, that is, that the practice of law is a professional business since we are engaged in an enterprise for profit. And since it is a business, the laws of economics apply: supply and demand, competition, cyclicity, etc. The exponent of all this is unceasing change that is evolutionary, like a climb up the phylogenetic tree. The future is no less bright for this change, but it is assuredly different.

Fortunately, changes have also been buffeting our clients' realities. Since clients are the *raison d'être* for practicing law, it is critical that we view them as the center of the marketing process. No sense practicing Neanderthal marketing in the age of computers.

Marketing, or business development, as a necessary function in the practice of law, is really about building these realities: a good client base, work you find interesting, and positive long-term relationships with clients who appreciate your efforts enough to return *and* refer others to you. As a professional practice, marketing is not about making cold calls and knocking on unwelcoming doors. Nor is it about throwing fistfuls of dollars at crassly commercial marketing tactics that degrade the stature of the profession — they don't work anyway. Professional marketing is about serving clients ethically while making a profit so that we can continue to practice and serve other clients.

While the emphasis of this book is geared to small firms and solo practitioners, the process I describe works in firms of any size. The focus is on maximizing your time to practice law by making intelligent, active, and personal marketing strategies a necessary but efficient adjunct to substantive matters. You will not be a marketing maven by the end of this book. But you will have a practical plan and tools you can use to forge ahead with the profitable growth of your practice.

A note on the genesis of my approach to marketing law firms is appropriate here. This book opens my professional toolbox to you. In the years that I have been running a marketing practice, I've had the chance to use these tools, sharpen them, and evaluate the results. They are presented here so that you do not have to reinvent the wheel.

In addition, when I work with firms large and small, I have the distinct pleasure of interviewing *their* clients — clients like yours — who have provided me with the best marketing advice. Their commentary is without doubt the *sine qua non* of marketing advice, and it is the true lens through which I view what works and what does not. Any reference I make to clients or interviewees is to fictionalized composites of reality, not real people. I offer the insights of this council of experts, along with my work in the field and the generous help of the contributing authors, and invite you to think along with me. Work on your dreams.

Christine Sandor Filip, Esq.
December, 1995

Table of Contents

Chapter One

Marketing Defined

MARKETING IS THE engine of enterprise. Like an engine, it works best when tuned up and fed good fuel so that it integrates smoothly with other parts of the car. Picture yourself in the driver's seat of your favorite vehicle humming along on a fine day with a clear map at your side. Your destination: the twin towns of Prosperity and Satisfaction. Really.

The first part of this book analyzes the parts of the engine, and since you're probably not a mechanical engineer, this analysis will most likely bore you. But, hang in there if you can. The parts are limited, and in truth it's the driver's intellect and judgment that really determine the success of the trip. Naming the parts, however, will make you a better driver and the trip considerably smoother. You might even bypass Dodge.

Parts is Parts

The classic definition of the marketing process is to find out what clients want and to deliver services that consistently meet those needs. The marketing engine has a limited number of parts: the *service* itself, *pricing, promotion* (selling, public relations, advertising, client communications) and the actual *delivery* of the service, called "channel of distribution." These are the "four Ps" (well, almost) of the marketing mix.

The way in which you synchronize these parts is important. If your marketing decisions were based on an honest evaluation of your marketplace and how it meshes with your professional competencies, the financial and qualitative results would probably be excellent. This good "fit" between your talents and the market's needs paves the way for what Harvard economist Michael Porter calls "sustainable competitive advantage," which, loosely translated, means above-average profitability. You might call it being at the right place at the right time with the right stuff, or maybe on the right road by way of careful planning. Competitive advantage, though, merits further discussion because it has financial and qualitative implications, which affect both you and your clients.

There are two pathways to competitive advantage (again, read profitability): (1) *low-cost production*, a profit path marked by charging average prices *and* continually pushing down the cost of production; and (2) the *differentiation* path, which allows you to increase your profits by communicating your unique attributes and charging a correlatively higher price. Don't get me wrong; you have to do both of these things to sustain profitability. But, trying to be all things to all people is a recipe for disaster. If you've analyzed your market, know your strengths and weaknesses, and know your work, one of these strategies should stand out as the best one for you to use.

Choosing one marketing strategy over another and following it is important for two primary reasons. First, defining your strategy, like choosing the best road, eliminates costly diversions. Second, defining your strategy forces you to evaluate your talents in light of your clients' needs and the terrain of the marketplace; in this sense, it is a critical learning experience. This type of analysis allows you to true up your course, readjust, and grow.

I remember seeing a televised interview with Broadway producer and dancer Tommy Tune. He was asked what separated him from other entertainers vying for the public spotlight — what made for his distinct success. He said that creating a production was like turning over a deck of cards for the audience. He remarked that he had the same deck of cards (talent) he'd always had, but experience had taught him many more ways to finesse the cards before the audience relative to timing, style, pace, and more. In the same vein, the critical analysis and self-evaluation that go into choosing a strategy will illuminate more variations and ultimately produce better results.

Choosing a Strategy

There are three business-related questions and one personal question that will assist you in choosing and defining your strategy:

1. **Firm Mission:** What resources (time, money, expertise, personnel) and disincentives (lack thereof) does my firm have that will facilitate or impede its success? Are the resources enough? If not, what alternatives are there? Are the disincentives fixable within the scope of our resources?
2. **Marketplace Data:** What target client needs must we address in order to be successful as a firm now and in the future? If you're experienced, you know that "target client needs" means focusing on the present and future needs of your *best* clients.
3. **Competitive Information:** How do we stack up against our finest competitors? Be stringently honest here, and ideally, ask a client to answer this question.
4. **Personal Issue:** What do you *like* to do?

Synthesizing your answers to these questions will help you define your strategic road map, whether you are an experienced practitioner or a neophyte.

The type of work you do may also help determine which strategy will work best for you. Uncomplicated divorces, real estate transactions, and personal bankruptcy work are examples of practice areas that may fit into a low-cost production strategy; if you can substitute less costly means of production, such as computers and/or people, and the work is volume driven, this strategy may be the most efficient.

As a practical matter, you still must have *some* element of differentiation lest your services appear to be a commodity. The point(s) of differentiation might be your location, hours of operation, a multilingual staff, or quick turnaround of work. Marketing investments are aimed at reducing costs while increasing volume.

Alternatively, a differentiation strategy relies on the communication of the unique benefits of a practice to attract clients willing to pay premium prices that drive profits. Labor-intensive, specialty practices such as patent law or complex litigation are susceptible to a differentiation strategy, since expertise is an inherent means of distinction. Again, this strategy must pay attention to driving down costs at the same time.

What is most important about whatever marketing strategy you choose is the consistent implementation of tactics which have been scrutinized for their congruence with your strategy. Both elements preserve your finite assets of time and money and can overcome even some of the most negative competitive forces — lower-priced competitors, steep learning curves, and demanding clients, to name a few.

Let's look at some quick examples of how the type of practice might influence choice of strategy and subsequent tactics. A lawyer with a commercial litigation practice or one with a patent specialty who chooses a differentiation strategy based on expertise levels would be better served by speaking or writing for industry groups (tactics) than by spending money on a large print ad (a low-cost producer tactic) in the Yellow Pages or a newspaper. Displaying competence through speaking engagements will take the patent lawyer or commercial litigator a lot further in promoting points of differentiation than an advertisement. Were the patent lawyer to spend most of his marketing expenses on an advertisement in a local paper, results probably would be poor. Consistent decisions, reliably executed, obviate unproductive marketing expenses.

Were you to have a resident marketing director, dealing with these decisions would be easy. Grafted on to the substantive work of being an attorney, all these pieces become onerous. For that reason, effective marketing tactics — ones that stimulate both business development and service quality — are in the foreground in this book. So it is that this book turns first to *personal* marketing strategies. Those are ones that showcase your talents, help you build long-lasting relationships with excellent clients, and generate the best payback.

Marketing Professional Services is Tricky

Lawyers function in the marketing universe of "professional services." Services alone, being intangible products and ephemeral, are hard enough to market. With the overlay of professional requirements, the business development function is even trickier. These twin requirements dictate very deliberate but different marketing actions than if one were marketing tangible goods, say, computers or office furniture.

Here are some special considerations to keep in mind as you master your own marketing fate:

1. Physical evidence works best because it gives prospects a way to "grasp" what you do and remember it. Put the evidence of your competence into tangible form whenever possible to accompany your sales pitch, whether one-on-one or to an audience. All these are tangible pieces of evidence: an engagement letter, a brochure, article reprint, newsletter, business card. Remember also that physical evidence to your prospects includes your office, treatment by you and your staff, and the timeliness and quality of your work product.
2. You have no stronger ally than a good reference. Prospective clients can't test-drive your services, nor do you want them to. Put them in contact with good, current clients as they evaluate whether to work with you.
3. Professional service relationships require maintenance. Once you have established the relationship, a periodic review will help the client remember the work and give you a common platform from which to contemplate future needs.

Why Marketing Counts

The goal of marketing is to create a "sale," or a decision in your favor. Inasmuch as this goal has a financial impact, it is equally important to recognize that good marketing has qualitative ramifications as well. Well thought out marketing that starts from your analysis of the fit between your competencies, the needs of prospective clients, and the landscape of your marketplace, all increase the probability of attracting the types of clients you want and can serve well. This good "fit" also means that these better clients will be happy with you, will refer others to you, and will come back to you in the future. Marketers call this result "quality."

But mostly, it means that by dint of forethought and analysis you will be able to consistently deliver what your best present and intended clients want.

In sum, the marketing process creates a decision point (a sale), and looks like this:

MARKETING ——> SALE = CLIENT CHOOSES YOU ——> FINANCIAL & QUALITATIVE IMPACT

The success of this process turns on matching your talents and competencies to the right target audience of prospective clients. This match positions you to communicate your unique advantages through a considered choice of marketing tactics so that a sale is more, rather than less, likely to happen.

Boosting Profitability

In pursuing the marketing-to-sales connection, choosing successful marketing tactics is easier if you pay attention to some economic ground rules that have grown out of research concerning client retention.[1] Without this economic insight, one might choose to spend money on marketing tactics that have small likelihood of success, and then generalize from invalid results. For example, a patent attorney who buys a costly ad space in a daily newspaper might see little return, even if the ad runs multiple times. Likewise, a business lawyer touting his or her services by sending letters to unknown business owners would have little likelihood of success. Both of these examples show disregard for the economic ground rules of managing client retention. Let's take a look at this important advice.

There are four ground rules that are critical:

1. Client loyalty or retention drives profitable growth, not sales volume, market share and other gauges of new client acquisition. *A 5 percent improvement in client retention can affect profits from 25 to 100 percent.*[2] Client loyalty or retention means getting *referrals, repurchases, cross-selling* opportunities, and *decreasing defections,* that is, clients who leave and never return.

   Referrals from present clients have a 92 percent loyalty rate versus a 68 percent rate for clients generated from advertising.
2. It is six times more expensive to get a new client than to retain an existing client, and new client acquisition will take you three times as long.[3] Continually focusing your marketing dollars on finding new clients is a very expensive, inefficient proposition. Twenty percent of your clients generate 80 percent of your fees.

3. A dissatisfied client will tell eight to ten other colleagues and friends about his unhappiness, and one in five will tell twenty.[4] As a result, your investments in marketing cannot overcome this impact.
4. Most clients will leave your practice because of perceived indifference, not fees.[5] The source of this "indifference" is usually inattention by you or a staff member — a question that lingers unanswered, a slow response to a phone call, a slow response to solving a problem that the client perceives as important, or brusque treatment from anyone at your firm.

The Implications of Client Retention Data

Taken to heart, these ground rules suggest that profitable growth comes from recurring work, referred clients, and the active management of preventing client defections. They also imply that if you know who your best clients are and why they selected you, then you have a profile of similarly situated prospective clients who are an additional, well-qualified target audience. Finally, by negative implication, the data says that continually going after new clients will undercut the profitable growth of your practice.

The shape of this more efficient marketing process is thus one of analysis (knowing who your best clients are) and creating effective two-way communication:

1. **Ask for information** — How are we doing? What else do you need? Who else can we serve?
2. **Give consultative information** — a newsletter, a briefing, a speech; hold a client function; or publish an article, all of which expand the horizon of relationships with present and prospective clients.
3. **Ensure an easy-to-use feedback loop** to each communication, whether face-to-face or in writing. Feedback loops can be surveys, questionnaires, fax back/mail back portions on newsletters, a pre-set time when a client is able to reach you by phone, quick response to complaints, informal focus groups, a "suggestion box" that staff can use to improve client services or operations, a follow-up phone call to a client. The ways to establish loops are end-less, but these loops are rarely adopted to the level of institutionalization. If they are, they become unique selling points for a firm.

In light of the economic suggestions of client retention, let's rework the two earlier examples of failed marketing tactics — the patent attorney and the business lawyer. The advertising campaign of the patent lawyer is unfocused because the readership is too general. While it might bring in some clients, they are not as worthy and well-qualified (68 percent loyalty rate from advertising versus the 92 percent rate from referrals), so the lawyer will spend time talking with marginal prospects and make clients out of very few. A better placement might be in a periodical read by his or her best clients, perhaps a scientific journal.

Advertising's effectiveness in persuading potential buyers is hard to document, but that aside, it is expensive in that it takes multiple exposures to bring in any number of worthwhile clients. Advertising execs talk about the "Rule of 7s," meaning that an ad should run at least seven times. If for that investment you bring in only marginally qualified prospective clients, the payback pales.

On the other hand, were the same patent attorney to speak at a conference attended by some of his or her best clients (a form of personal marketing strategy), there would more likely be credible results. Using good clients' affiliation groups to focus the marketing steps showcases the attorney's competence to a very well-qualified audience: There are both clients and similarly situated non-clients in that audience. Pulling in new business through this target market enhances quality because the audience's needs match the competence of the attorney.

Choosing to structure your marketing program around the principles of managing client retention obviates empty results, and targets the kind of growth that has both profitability and quality enhancements unattainable through conventional marketing tactics.

If you are just starting a practice, your targeted best "clients" should be defined by research, even if only informal. Talk to and solicit advice from lawyers with the type of practice you would like to start. Then do some research on your own at your local library to refine your target audience: Where do they live and work? What do they read? What are their issues?

The next question is what one should do to harness the client retention process without having a marketing maven on staff and without spending a fortune.

The Structural Implications of Client Retention

If taken seriously for their financial and qualitative implications, the economic principles set forth above will cause you to spend time and money in new ways. To put our intellectual arms around this process, it's easiest to discuss the structural implications of managing retention. They are: Divide your client base into three groups (levels one, two, and three, described in subsequent pages); spend your time and money on your top clients and their clones; and stop spending time and money on your least profitable clients.

Analyzing Your Client Base: Boring but Necessary

Have you ever listened to a dynamic speaker and felt alone in the room, like the speaker was talking directly to you? Analyzing your client base has the same effect: Understanding the needs and attributes of clients allows you to communicate efficiently and persuasively. The analysis process can induce narcolepsy even in compulsive learners, but once done, you will have a motherlode of information to speed marketing results.

Your client base — that is, the clients you now serve and have served in the last two to three years — should be divided, or segmented, into three groups using *profitability* and some other defining criteria: Level One clients are *profitable*, pay on time, and bring work you enjoy. What else do you know about them that can help sort them out (age, occupation, education, etc.)?

Level Two clients are *marginally profitable*, but some are susceptible to expansion or are fertile referral sources. They may have great contacts. Level Three clients are those who (by popular vote) you don't want repeat business from because they are not profitable, pay slowly, bring you the wrong type of work, or demand too much. The challenge is to identify them before they become clients.

In doing this analysis, you should note two generalities: (1) Level Ones are approximately 20 percent of your base, but generate close to 80 percent of your fees; and (2) you probably spend a lot of your time with unproductive Level Twos and Threes. They call on you even when they haven't paid their bills.

If your next, excellent clients come from the ranks of your Level One base, the marketing choices defined as good "investments" will change.

Investment Priorities

Client Levels	Marketing Tactics
Level One	Spend your marketing dollars here by creating opportunities to cross-sell, get referrals and repeat purchases — implement client functions, create interactive communications, and enhance service offerings. Ask these clients' advice and their evaluations; become enmeshed in *their* networks.
Level Two	Select a small number of these clients whom you feel are expandable or who are gatekeepers to fertile networks of peers. Treat them like Level Ones.

Level Three Note how you got these clients and do not repeat this pattern. The pattern may have to do with some professional status, such as being members of a particular industry, or some other personal status, which makes for a poor working relationship.

Stopping Defections Among Level One Clients

As noted earlier, stopping defections is equally as important to profitable growth as assertively managing client retention or loyalty. Having one of your best clients exit your practice will make for a bad day at Blackrock. Here are some tips:

1. **Clients don't leave because of fees.** They leave because of *indifference by you or someone on your staff.* Since these experiences are entirely controllable, it's critical to understand why clients leave. *If you ask,* you will get some very concrete examples. Most times, clients will leave *without* complaining, so unless you inquire, you can't take remedial action.
2. **When clients complain, fix it fast.** Your response time to client dissatisfaction is very important. If you can resolve the basis for complaint *within 24 hours,* the client will remain loyal (and profitable). Your staff should be able to launch a *Problem Alert* form and get the *attention and action of the most senior person involved.*
3. **What do clients complain about?** Usually it's slow response times, or they have misconceptions about the requirements of your work. The work process of professionals is "invisible"— clients see the end product, not the hours of research, learning, and thought. Frequently, clients think you have *breached your ethical responsibilities when you've missed deadlines or not explained delays.* Be clear about your time commitments with clients and explain what goes into your work in plain terms.

Target Marketing

The phrase "target marketing" classically means defining your marketing prospects at the beginning of the marketing planning process. Inasmuch as most practitioners already have a client base, for the purpose of our discussion, targeting your best client prospects can be defined from within the ranks of your Level One clients and their *clones* — similar prospects you don't yet know — and *analogues*, who have some similarity, but are slightly different.

One further set of variables divides your base into two important categories:

1. Clients who are *individual* buyers of legal services, and
2. Clients who represent *businesses* or other entities.

The reason that we separate these two groups within the Level One segment is that they usually have different needs, or reasons why they come to you. As a result, defining them by their needs (and hence their buying criteria) helps make the marketing process more efficient.

For example, the fact that your institutional or business buyers come from one particular industry, say regional beverage bottlers, might suggest a number of efficient, new marketing tactics. You might find that the bottlers have a trade association in which there are opportunities for you to give a seminar or write for the association newsletter. As a result of these marketing tactics, your firm would be introduced to a host of other good prospective clients who have legal needs that you are comfortable serving.

Similarly, on the individual buyer level, you might find that many of your clients came to you because of your participation in community, social, or religious organizations, or that they can be defined by some personal characteristic or status such as residence, age, income level, or where they live. In knowing, for instance, that many of your individual clients came to you from a particular community, you would then be able to target your marketing tactics to that specific geographic area, such as running seminars in a community organization or writing an article for a local newspaper rather than for a trade journal or industry newsletter.

Dividing your Level One group into segments that identify them allows you to communicate and to market to them more efficiently, thereby driving down your marketing expenses. Once you can describe major variables among your best clients, you will then be able to see how to reach them effectively to encourage repeat business, referrals, and new matters. These Level One segment groups also help you forecast future results since you have some knowledge and a track record from past experience. This predictive capability will help you forecast revenue growth, anticipate staffing and technology requirements, and add more certainty to your business plan.

The major segment variables among your Level Ones are:

Individual Buyers	Institutional/Business Buyers
Age	Industry – SIC codes
Income	Geographic location
Residence	Benefits sought
Education	Size of entity
Occupation	Number of employees
Offspring	Regulatory environment
Lifestyle	Retail/wholesale
Values	Distributor
	Profit/non-profit

Once you have segmented your Level One clients into groups, you can begin to target your marketing efforts by asking yourself the following questions:

1. *How else can I serve these clients?* Do they need enhanced or subsequent services? Result: more business from present clients and cross-selling opportunities.
2. *How can I encourage referrals from these clients?* Result: new business opportunities that are likely to be good, well-qualified and, hence, produce loyal new clients.
3. *What other potential clients are similar to my present clients?* Result: new business prospects that have similar needs and therefore are a good fit to my present competencies.

You may find that you have a group of Level One clients who have nothing more in common than residence in a geographic area — firms with a general practice usually. That you have only one segment variable, namely, geographic location, is still worthwhile. With that, you can target your marketing efforts to geographic parameters, such as by attending civic events and organizations, taking an active role in community groups, writing or advertising in a local paper, becoming a political candidate, or attending meetings of local business organizations.

"My Clients Are Different," You Say

A seeming roadblock in using segmentation variables to describe your Level One clients is the appearance of one-time-only clients who seem to have no further need for your services. This may be true, but further analysis can lead you to think about subsequent services or remarketing to the sources who provided the original referrals.

Let's take a look at a one-time-only client base. In a solo practice that focused on personal bankruptcy, there seemed, on first analysis, to be no potential for more business. The client base analysis revealed that clients came primarily from one county, and many of them had filed for bankruptcy protection a year or two before. One could assume that this client base was not susceptible to further marketing efforts. However, to find out more, the attorney and I created a survey form (see p. 71) and sent it to this client base. In the form we asked whether, in addition to the services they had used previously, these individuals knew about other practice areas and services that the lawyer offered. Additionally, we suggested that life changes such as births, marriage, divorce, and the like were appropriate times to consult an attorney. Finally, we informed the client that the attorney would be giving free public seminars on the subject of debtor/creditor relationships. The survey went out by mail with a stamped, self-addressed envelope, and we provided the fax number of the attorney so that, alternatively, the client could fax the survey back.

More than one-third of the recipients responded. The survey brought in substantial new and follow-up service opportunities. Contrary to the original assumption that individuals who file personal bankruptcies do not have subsequent legal needs, we found that their lives brought them to new junctures requiring new services, and that they were viable referral sources — their community and familial contacts were abundant.

What marketing tactics did we then implement? First, those who had current needs were phoned by the attorney, and consultations were set up. Second, the referrals were contacted. Third, in looking at viable ways to communicate with the larger community audiences, the attorney set up a number of seminars in local public libraries on issues of debtor/creditor relationships. Far from being a deadbeat marketing proposition, this one-time-only client base was fertile ground. This marketing exercise had a secondary gain for the solo practitioner: It allowed the attorney financial breathing room to develop other practice areas because of the increase in fee generation from Level One clients.

Summary

The most profitable way to grow your practice is to focus your marketing investments on your Level One client base, target specific Level Two clients for expansion, and decrease the burden of dealing with Level Three clients by not repeating the pattern that brought them to your practice. The economic proposition that supports this Level One focus is that from small changes (5 percent) in your retention and cultivation of Level Ones springs an enormous change in profitability (from 25 to 100 percent). In other words, by aiming your marketing dollars at fertile targets, you get the best payback in financial terms and in the quality of work, because there's a good fit with your competencies. Remember, your Level Ones usually are 20 percent of your base, but generate up to 80 percent of your fees. Marketing to Level Ones produces repurchases, referrals, and a bridge to similarly situated prospective clients, dubbed "clones" and "analogues."

The broad analysis outlined:

Segregate clients ——> Levels One, Two, Three	**Segment Level Ones ——> into efficient groups**	**Target your markets**
Levels describe profitability and some other variables, such as practice areas and services needed	Segments describe individuals vs. institutional buyers to help you notice commonalities and plan efficient tactics	Segments can be profiled for easier marketing

This analysis moves you from merely mulling over what to do about business development to embarking on a course of very efficient action. However, the most difficult part of getting the results you want *is* moving into action — the tactical marketing phase. But if you know who your best clients are, and you know how to reach them efficiently, the results will turn solely on your willingness to do what we'll discuss in the next chapters.

There are two very important secondary gains that you will realize from this referral-based business development model: First, when you attract business from your best clients and similarly situated prospects, you minimize your time and expenses. This occurs because the work you bring in fits with your competencies and, as a result, costs you less to produce. Second, and springing from this good fit between you and the client, the probability of disputes and misunderstandings will also decrease. When this happens, "quality" is the result.

In simple terms, "quality" is the alignment of your practice to deliver what your Level Ones want on a consistent basis. This model of business development allows you to rediscover what your best clients want, and to focus your marketing tactics to meet those needs.

Writing a Marketing Plan

Putting your marketing plan in print breathes life into your intentions and helps you to keep your efforts on track. Although later on in this book I will give you an abbreviated version called a Marketing Action Planner, which helps plot out your tactics in a calendar format, you may want to do a more extensive version. The outline on the following pages will lead you through the more extensive process.

WRITING YOUR MARKETING PLAN

A GOOD MARKETING PLAN:

1. PRESENTS IDEAS LOGICALLY AND CLEARLY.

2. INCORPORATES ALL AVAILABLE, PERTINENT DATA.

3. OUTLINES DECISIONS REFLECTING A FIRM'S MISSION STATEMENT.

4. SETS REALISTIC GOALS ACHIEVABLE WITHIN THE ESTABLISHED TIME FRAMEWORK.

5. PROVIDES A GUIDELINE FOR A FIRM'S ACTIONS.

6. PERMITS CHANGE IF EXTRAORDINARY EVENTS DICTATE.

7. IS IN WRITING SO YOU WON'T FORGET IMPORTANT DUTIES AND DECISIONS.

CONTENT OF THE PLAN

EXECUTIVE SUMMARY

MISSION STATEMENT

SITUATION ANALYSIS

- The Firm
- The Market (Share, Trends, Potential, Segmentation, Environment)
- The Product(s) and/or Service(s)
- The Competition
- Pricing
- Personnel
- Client Needs and Problems
- Marketing Communications

ASSUMPTIONS AND TRENDS

MARKETING OPPORTUNITIES

GOALS

STRATEGY

TACTICS

ACTION PLAN: ALLOCATING/PLANNING/SCHEDULING RESOURCES

FORECAST/BUDGET

RISKS/CONTINGENCY PLANS AND ALTERNATIVE ACTIONS

THE MISSION STATEMENT

1. WHAT YOUR FIRM WANTS TO BE WHEN IT GROWS UP.
2. A BROAD FRAMEWORK THAT ESTABLISHES THE SCOPE FOR PRESENT FUNCTIONS AND FUTURE DEVELOPMENT.
3. THE MISSION STATEMENT MUST DIRECT THE FIRM'S OPERATING UNITS OR PRACTICE AREAS.
4. TRADITIONALLY, THE STATEMENT FOCUSES ON THE ENTIRE FIRM.

EXAMPLES OF A MISSION STATEMENT:

SMITH AND BALL IS A LABOR AND EMPLOYMENT FIRM THAT COMPREHENSIVELY REPRESENTS UNIONS AND INDIVIDUALS IN THEIR RELATIONSHIPS WITH EMPLOYERS.

HOW WOULD YOU WRITE THE MISSION STATEMENT FOR YOUR FIRM?

SPECIFY IF FOR THE FIRM, A PRACTICE AREA, OR YOU.

MISSION STATEMENT:

SITUATION ANALYSIS

COORDINATES ALL AVAILABLE, RELEVANT INFORMATION GATHERED THROUGH ALL POSSIBLE RESEARCH RESOURCES.

A. YOUR FIRM

1. WHERE IS THE FIRM NOW?
2. WHAT ARE ITS STRENGTHS AND WEAKNESSES?
3. WHAT IS YOUR RETENTION RATE?

B. THE MARKETS

1. WHAT IS YOUR PRIMARY MARKET?
2. WHAT IS ITS SIZE?
3. HOW WOULD YOU DESCRIBE YOUR CLIENTS IN THIS MARKET? (LEVELS 1-3, SEGMENTS?) WHERE ARE THEY, AND WHAT ARE THEIR NEEDS?
4. HOW WOULD YOU DESCRIBE YOUR CLIENT POTENTIAL?
5. HOW WOULD YOU DEFINE THE CURRENT AND POTENTIAL MARKET SEGMENTS? QUANTIFY THOSE MARKETS IN TERMS OF BENEFITS, DEMOGRAPHICS OR OTHER VARIABLES.
6. WHAT IS THE STANDARD/ TYPICAL BUYING CYCLE FOR YOUR SERVICE? DESCRIBE IT AND INCLUDE METHODS OF HOW YOUR FIRM DOES BUSINESS.

C. PRODUCT(S)/ SERVICE(S)

1. HOW WOULD YOU DEFINE ITS UNIQUE BENEFITS AND FEATURES? PROVIDE A BRIEF HISTORY OF YOUR SERVICES. INCLUDE ANY OBJECTIONS TO IT.
2. WHAT IS ITS PRICE IN RELATION TO ITS PERCEIVED BENEFITS? TO ITS FUTURE POTENTIAL?
3. WHAT IS YOUR CURRENT METHOD OF MARKETING? HOW SUCCESSFUL IS THIS METHOD? HOW DOES IT WORK?

D. SALES AND MARKETING

1. DESCRIBE YOUR RAINMAKERS: NUMBER OF PEOPLE, EFFECTIVENESS, SALES SKILLS, COST OF SALES, STRENGTHS OR WEAKNESSES.

E. PROFITABILITY

1. HOW DOES ACTUAL PROFIT COMPARE TO LAST YEAR'S FORECAST? WHAT REASONS WOULD YOU GIVE?
2. ANALYZE THE PERFORMANCE OF EACH SERVICE OR PRACTICE AREA.
3. ANALYZE PROFITABILITY IN TERMS OF YOUR "SALES TEAMS" AND YOUR CLIENTS.
4. ANALYZE YOUR COMMUNICATIONS: WHAT KIND OF PUBLIC RELATIONS, ADVERTISING, AND MARKETING COMMUNICATIONS DID YOU USE? WERE THEY EFFECTIVE?
5. WHAT IS YOUR CLIENT RETENTION RATE YEAR TO YEAR?

F. COMPETITION

1. WHO ARE YOUR COMPETITORS?
2. HOW DO YOU RANK THEM?
3. CAN YOU FORESEE NEW COMPETITORS FOR THE COMING YEAR?
4. DESCRIBE YOUR COMPETITORS' SERVICES AND PRACTICE AREAS.
5. HOW MUCH DETAIL CAN YOU PROVIDE WITH GOOD CERTAINTY?
6. IS NEW TECHNOLOGY A COMPETITOR?

G. ECONOMIC ANALYSIS

PROJECT LIKELY DEVELOPMENTS WHICH COULD SPECIFICALLY IMPACT YOUR MARKET.

1. SOCIAL
2. TECHNICAL
3. ECONOMIC
4. REGULATORY
5. COMPETITIVE

VERIFYING YOUR INFORMATION

HARD VS. SOFT FACTS

1. THE MARKETING PLAN MUST BE BASED ON FACTS, NOT HUNCHES.

2. KNOW WHAT INFORMATION IS AVAILABLE AND WHERE TO FIND IT.

3. A SIX-STEP, COMMON-SENSE APPROACH:
   - Decide what information firm personnel can obtain
   - Give specific assignments in-house
   - Reinforce the importance of accurate information
   - Set deadlines
   - Review the results
   - Use an outside consultant:

     — when insiders don't have the time or special skills

     — to confirm data collected by your own people

ASSUMPTIONS AND TRENDS

SCENARIO PLANNING

I'M ABSOLUTELY CERTAIN OF . . . BUT WHAT IF . . .? THEN WHAT . . .?

A. MARKETS ARE NEVER STATIC

DEEP IN OUR BRAINS WE UNCONSCIOUSLY ASSUME THAT MARKET FACTORS WILL NOT CHANGE.

THIS IS ALWAYS WRONG.

B. MARKET REALITIES ARE FULL OF SURPRISES

DESPITE OUR FONDEST HOPES TO THE CONTRARY, UNFORESEEN EVENTS ALWAYS AFFECT RESULTS.

GIVEN THE FOREGOING, PREPARATION OF THE MARKETING PLAN SHOULD INCLUDE "WHAT IF" SCENARIO PLANNING FOR ALL MAJOR OPERATING ASSUMPTIONS.

1. WHAT ARE TWO EVENTS DURING THE NEXT 12 MONTHS THAT COULD POSSIBLY IMPACT YOUR MARKETING ACTIVITIES?

   POSITIVE IMPACT:

   NEGATIVE IMPACT:

2. WHAT ARE TWO MARKET FACTORS MOST CERTAIN TO REMAIN THE SAME?

   1. ______________________________

      ____

   2. ______________________________

      ____

MARKETING OPPORTUNITIES

CONSIDERING YOUR MARKETING REALITIES AND YOUR RESOURCES, WHAT OPPORTUNITIES SHOULD YOU TAKE TO BE MORE SUCCESSFUL THIS YEAR?

LIST EACH OPPORTUNITY AND HOW YOUR FIRM WILL CAPTURE IT:

1. ____

2. ____

3. ____

MARKETING GOALS

1. EACH GOAL SHOULD BE DESIGNED IN THE CONTEXT OF THE MISSION STATEMENT.
2. EACH GOAL SHOULD BE FOCUSED AND SPECIFIC.
3. GOALS CAN SERVE AS PERFORMANCE CRITERIA BY:
    - identifying important issues
    - quantifying performance expectations
    - focusing attention on important issues
    - being totally unambiguous

EXAMPLES OF MARKETING GOALS

1. INCREASE THE NUMBER OF NET NEW CLIENTS IN SEGMENT ONE BY 10%.
2. INCREASE REVENUES BY 2% PER QUARTER.
3. COMPLETE A CLIENT SATISFACTION SURVEY IN THE FIRST QUARTER AND USE THE RESULTS TO INCREASE CLIENT ACCEPTANCE RATES BY 3.5% PER QUARTER.
4. INCREASE NEW CLIENT WORK AT ACCEPTABLE MARGINS (41%) 7% BY YEAR END.

HOW STRATEGY FUNCTIONS IN THE MARKETING PLAN

Strategy is a planned, comprehensive approach to facilitating the careful use of finite resources (money, time, energy) in order to get the highest return on investment.

In marketing terms, there are two main strategies: *differentiation and low-cost producer. Differentiation* means that the firm communicates real and substantial points of difference between their products and those of the competition. As a result, the firm is able to capture better-than-average margins on the service product sold; the value of the firm's unique attributes justifies the premium price. The success of the *low-cost producer* depends on continuous decreases in the cost of production and at least average prices.

Although neither strategy can be used exclusively, one strategy should prevail in order to reap the benefits of consistent decision making. A firm that consistently makes marketing decisions that support its strategy will realize better returns than one that employs a scattered approach.

A firm that has chosen differentiation must still pay attention to decreasing the costs of production, and the same is true for low-cost producers. Marketing failures occur when firms try to be all things to their clients. As a result, no clear market identity or "position" is established in the buyers' minds.

There is one last variant on strategy: When either differentiation or low-cost production is aimed at a small slice of the potential market, the strategy is called a *focus* strategy. One, therefore, can have a focus strategy based on either differentiation or low-cost production.

DIFFERENTIATION STRATEGY

A. RATIONALE

1. THERE ARE NO COMMODITIES
2. ALL GOODS AND SERVICES CAN BE DIFFERENTIATED TO DISTINGUISH YOUR PRODUCTS FROM THOSE OFFERED BY YOUR COMPETITORS
3. NOTHING IS EXEMPT FROM CONSIDERATION

B. MEANS OF DIFFERENTIATION

1. IDENTIFIABLE VISUALLY
2. MEASURABLE
3. IMPLIED
4. CLAIMED
5. CAN BE PART OF THE TANGIBLE PRODUCT (E.G., A WRITTEN ESTATE PLAN) OR PART OF THE SERVICE THAT ENHANCES THE PRODUCT
6. MUST HAVE **VALUE** TO THE CLIENT

C. INFLUENCE OF PRICE

PRICE IS RARELY THE ISSUE. IN HIGHLY COMPETITIVE INDUSTRIES, THE FOLLOWING SEQUENCE USUALLY OCCURS:

1. PRICE IS VISIBLE
2. OTHER POSSIBILITIES ARE PUT ASIDE
3. NOTHING ELSE IS OFFERED
4. PRICE BECOMES THE ONLY VARIABLE LEFT TO THE CLIENT

IT IS BECAUSE PRICE IS SO VISIBLE AND EASILY MEASURED THAT IT TOO OFTEN DEFLECTS ATTENTION FROM OTHER BUYING CRITERIA WHICH ARE EQUALLY IMPORTANT IN THE BUYERS' MINDS, SUCH AS RESPONSIVE SERVICE.

LOW-COST PRODUCTION

A. THE SUCCESS OF LOW-COST PRODUCER STRATEGY DEPENDS ON:

1. THE FIRM'S SCOPE OF SEGMENTS SERVED
2. LOW OVERHEAD
3. LOW-COST LABOR, OR THE SUBSTITUTION OF TECHNOLOGY TO DECREASE PRODUCTION COSTS
4. EFFECTIVE TRAINING AND MANAGEMENT PROCEDURES
5. TAKING ADVANTAGE OF ALL COST RESOURCES

B. REQUIREMENTS

1. LARGE MARKET SHARE FOR LOWER PURCHASING COSTS
2. ECONOMIES AND EFFICIENCIES IN PRODUCTION
3. TIGHT COST AND OVERHEAD CONTROLS
4. FREQUENT, DETAILED CONTROL REPORTS
5. STRUCTURED ORGANIZATION AND RESPONSIBILITIES
6. INCENTIVES BASED ON COST-EFFICIENT PRODUCTION
7. MAINTENANCE OF TECHNOLOGICAL CAPABILITIES

C. INITIAL INVESTMENT

1. PURCHASE OF STATE-OF-THE-ART EQUIPMENT
2. DEVELOPMENT OF TECHNOLOGY
3. AGGRESSIVE PRICE SETTING
4. SUFFICIENT CAPITALIZATION TO DEAL WITH START-UP AND OPERATING COSTS

GENERAL RULES OF SUCCESSFUL MARKETING

1. SELF-SERVING PRESENTATIONS AND MARKETING COMMUNICATIONS DO NOT SELL. CLIENTS BUY FOR BENEFITS, THAT IS, WHAT THE PRODUCT/SERVICE WILL DO FOR THEM.
2. IF VALUE IS NOT DELIVERED CONSISTENTLY, CLIENTS WILL SWITCH — USUALLY FASTER THAN YOU THINK.
3. WHAT THE CLIENTS VALUE, HOW THEY RANK THEIR BUYING CRITERIA, SHOULD BE THE SUBJECT OF CONSTANT RESEARCH BY THE FIRM. THIS RESEARCH NEED NOT BE FORMAL; IT CAN BE AS INFORMAL AS FACE-TO-FACE CONVERSATION WITH YOUR CLIENTS.
4. THE REAL NEEDS YOU ARE MEETING WITH YOUR SERVICES ARE FREQUENTLY NOT OBVIOUS, AND THEY MAY CHANGE OVER TIME.
5. THE MORE INFORMATION YOU HAVE ABOUT YOUR CLIENTS AND WHY THEY BUY YOUR SERVICES, THE MORE SUCCESSFUL YOU WILL BE IN THE MARKET.

MARKETING GOALS: A PRACTICAL APPROACH

I. PROCESS

1. GOALS ARE A MAJOR FACTOR IN THE MARKETING PLAN. THEY ARE THE TARGETS TOWARD WHICH THE FIRM AND INDIVIDUALS WILL WORK THROUGHOUT THE YEAR. *MARKETING GOALS SHOULD BE CONSISTENT WITH AND SHOULD CARRY OUT THE MARKETING STRATEGY.*

2. GOALS SHOULD BE BOTH REALISTIC AND AMBITIOUS. IT IS BEST TO SET GOALS THROUGH INTERACTIVE GROUP PROCESS.

3. GOALS SERVE MULTIPLE PURPOSES:

   A. PROVIDE INCENTIVES AND MOTIVATION

   B. ESTABLISH CRITERIA FOR JUDGING PERFORMANCE LEVELS OF OPERATING UNITS AND INDIVIDUALS

   C. AVOID UNCERTAINTY — ONE OF THE MOST NEGATIVE WORKING CONDITIONS

   D. IDENTIFY SUPERIOR PERFORMANCE

   E. SERVE AS A COMMUNICATION MECHANISM BETWEEN PARTNERS, ASSOCIATES, AND STAFF

4. GOALS SHOULD INCLUDE:

   A. CONCRETE RESULTS

   B. A TIMETABLE FOR PERFORMANCE

   C. ASSIGNED RESPONSIBILITY

5. AS STATEMENTS OF RESULTS, GOALS ENCOMPASS NUMEROUS SUPPORTIVE MARKETING TACTICS. BECAUSE OF THIS, IT IS WISE TO SET ONLY TWO OR THREE GOALS PER PLANNING PERIOD.

6. ALL EMPLOYEES AND JOB FUNCTIONS CAN BE INCLUDED IN THE PROCESS.

II. SIX STEPS

1. IDENTIFY AND DEFINE THE AREAS INCLUDED IN THE MARKETING PLAN.
2. ASSIGN RESPONSIBILITY FOR EACH AREA TO SPECIFIC INDIVIDUALS.
3. CARRY OUT GOAL SETTING BEFORE THE ANNUAL BUDGET IS PREPARED SO THAT RESOURCES WILL BE ALLOCATED TO ACHIEVE THE GOALS.
4. SET CONCRETE, ACHIEVABLE, MEASURABLE GOALS.
5. CONDUCT PERIODIC EVALUATION SESSIONS.
6. SET NEW GOALS AND CONTINUE THE PROCESS.

BUILD ON THE MISSION STATEMENT YOU HAVE WRITTEN

SPECIFY TWO MARKETING GOALS:

GOAL #1:

____

____

____

____

____

GOAL #2:

____

____

____

____

____

TEST EACH FOR INTERNAL CONSISTENCY:

GOAL 1 MESHES WITH THE MISSION STATEMENT BECAUSE:

____

____

____

____

GOAL 2 MESHES WITH THE MISSION STATEMENT BECAUSE:

____

____

____

____

MARKETING TACTICS

MARKETING TACTICS ARE THE ACTIONS WHICH ADVANCE YOUR MARKETING GOALS.

TACTICS SHOULD BE CONSISTENT WITH EACH MARKETING GOAL AND SHOULD DETAIL THE ACTIONS NECESSARY TO ACCOMPLISH THE GOAL.

TACTICS SHOULD:

1. BE ASSIGNED TO SPECIFIC PEOPLE.
2. HAVE TARGET COMPLETION DATES.
3. HAVE EVALUATION DATES AND METHODOLOGIES BUILT IN.

TACTICS MAY:

1. BE ORGANIZED BY REVENUE RESULTS, PRACTICE AREAS, OFFICES, OR ATTORNEYS.
2. INCLUDE BUDGET TARGETS FOR REVENUES AND EXPENSES.
3. NECESSITATE OTHER MARKETING ACTIONS, SUCH AS PUBLIC RELATIONS, ADVERTISING, SEMINARS, ETC.
4. REQUIRE TRAINING.
5. INCLUDE PRICING/PAYMENT TERM CONSIDERATIONS.
6. NECESSITATE ORGANIZATIONAL CHANGES SUCH AS HIRING, MERGER, OR DOWNSIZING.

Endnotes

1. Frederick F. Reicheld and W. Earl Sasser, "Zero Defections: Quality Comes to Service," *Harvard Business Review*, September 1992, p. 105. J. L. Heskett, L. A. Schlesinger, et al., "Putting the Service-Profit Chain to Work," *Harvard Business Review*, March 1994, p. 164.

2. *Ibid*, Reicheld and Sasser, p. 105-7.

3. Patricia Sellers, "Keeping the Buyers You Already Have," *Fortune*, Autumn-Winter, 1993, p. 56-60.

4. John Goodman, Technical Assistance Research Programs, Inc., "Measuring the Grapevine, Consumers Response and Word of Mouth," 1986.

5. *U.S. News and World Report*, Nov. 11, 1991.

Chapter Two

Personal Marketing Strategies

WITH THE ANALYSIS of your present or prospective client base completed, choosing which marketing tactics to implement is important. We start with personal marketing tactics first, as opposed to firm-wide tactics, because of their primacy to growth and professional reputation.

Personal marketing tactics use you — your competence and skills — as the focus of business development. There are two reasons that personal tactics are a priority: (1) since you are the product that prospective clients "buy," greater exposure to potential clients yields faster marketing results than firm-wide strategies, such as a brochure; and (2) personal marketing tactics are the most professional way to market — their intended consequences are enhanced relationships with present and prospective clients, and you are in control.

This chapter shows you how to put personal marketing tactics to work for you today.

I recently met with a law school colleague of mine to analyze her client base into the three levels. She had a growing litigation practice, but complained that her weeks were overcrowded with evening meetings, bad chicken dinners, and fearsome rooms full of unknown people. She was tired. Could I help? Her practice presents a model for marketing to both individuals and business entities — a how-to for implementing personal marketing tactics to Level One clients to encourage the profitable and timely growth of a practice.

From Analysis to Action

Interestingly, we noticed a knot of clients from a specific industry (office equipment dealers) with whom my friend Betsy had worked for years, and a growing number of individuals who sought Betsy's advice to negotiate severance packages with their soon-to-be former employers.

A seemingly disparate group, being institutional clients and individuals, but they both utilized her expert negotiation and litigation skills. These skills were, in fact, the source of Betsy's differentiation — she got good results very efficiently. In the severance setting, she worked aggressively to position her clients for future success and employability by keeping them out of court and out of the press. In litigation, her fine research and strategy skills kept her adversaries off balance. Betsy was usually better prepared than her opponents.

Since the office equipment dealers made up the largest piece of her client base, we turned our attention there first. What had she been doing with these Level One clients to serve their needs better so that recurring business, cross-selling, and referrals grew? Not much. It appeared that this group of clients was seeking to diminish the use of outside counsel, so Betsy thought that her time was better spent on the business, community and professional evening meeting trail, trying to make contacts with other potential new clients — networking, in other words. Hence the chicken dinner complaints. Betsy was worn out from the constant need to be "on" at these evening events after rigorous days of work. Few new clients were emerging from this tiresome process, and she felt boxed in by the lack of results.

This snapshot of Betsy's practice is illustrative of many others: a small firm or solo practice with some individual and some corporate or institutional clients, I often hear complaints from this type of practitioner, who feels too small to do any "real" marketing to present or prospective clients. "Real" marketing is assumed to mean brochures, advertising, lavish client functions. The stuff of dreams for most small practices.

Marketing, however, functions on two levels: the personal side of marketing, which is often called networking or rainmaking (when it works), and firm-wide marketing, which includes brochures, advertising, and public relations. Because these tactics represent the firm, not the attorneys, to the outside world, and because firm-wide marketing is perceived to be the real stuff, many attorneys feel that absent the ability to sink lots of dollars into this type of enterprise, their marketing efforts are for naught.

That notion is erroneous for a variety of reasons. Level One clients have told me in interview after interview that they choose you because of who you are, not what you know. In fact, most clients, no matter how sophisticated, do not know how to evaluate your expertise or credentials other than to rely on a colleague's attestation of your good work — a reference, in other words — coupled with their gut feelings. They rely most heavily on how they feel about you when they talk to you. Do they feel comfortable with you; do you seem interested in them as persons; do you seem to be the kind of lawyer who will work well with them, take action, and communicate well? They evaluate your expertise through the prism of interpersonal characteristics and first impressions, none of which can be adequately portrayed through brochures, advertising, or public relations.

Because good clients choose *you*, personal marketing strategies in the form of client functions and communication programs, networking, public speaking, and article publication have to be the first concern. They are the best vehicles to deliver the information clients use to select counsel. Firm-wide marketing activities cannot substitute for the personal side of marketing because they are impersonal portrayals of your expertise. Professional-level marketing is at its heart a process of affiliation and relationship building. Results stem from increasing your connectedness to clearly defined target markets.

Back to Betsy

But let's go back to my friend Betsy. She was doing a lot of personal marketing but with very slow results. What was wrong with her activities?

Betsy had ruled out personal marketing to her best target audience, that is, the office equipment dealers, because of their stated policy to attempt to decrease their reliance on outside counsel.

In short, Betsy was getting slow results because she was not spending her marketing time increasing her affiliation to this group. She should have been keeping in touch with them by doing anything from having a cup of coffee or lunch, to holding an executive briefing (the topic might be how to use outside counsel cost-effectively), even if just for two people. The goal of such activities is to increase the two-way communication between attorney and client. Being the professional, it's up to Betsy to initiate this process.

That the client wanted to decrease the use of outside counsel (read, pay less) is not a new notion, so here are some ideas about how Betsy can proceed. By taking the first step in suggesting a forum on "managing outside counsel," Betsy would have the first-mover advantage of being able to shape the discussion, perhaps not leading to the presumed result of taking a hit on fees, but to renovating the working relationship and uncovering other ways to be of service.

In addition to this forum, Betsy could have sent a short newsletter on the same subject to dealers she could not meet with, clients and prospects alike. Seminar and newsletter topics have to fit clients' needs, in essence, help them be more successful, but these can also stimulate client interest in other areas of potential work: how to avoid employment litigation; hiring, management, and firing policies; how to negotiate better contracts with suppliers; and on and on. All of these topics address how to save the owners money.

Betsy Gets Connected

Betsy rarely attended the regional trade association meetings of equipment dealers, assuming that they were not good prospects for work. But Betsy's tenure with this industry group should have earned her a speaking engagement with their trade association, or alternatively, the publication of an article in the association's newsletter.

She could address how to utilize outside counsel efficiently, or another timely topic. By putting her expertise in that forum, Betsy would expose herself to many *similarly situated* prospects who might seize the opportunity to switch to more cost-conscious counsel. This exposure would work to enhance her perceived expertise and success — being that she is a speaker and writer. Clients and prospects want to work with successful people.

Finally, Betsy might have asked herself, what other industries are clones or analogues of this one? Which ones have similar legal issues because their industry structure is similar? For example, such similar industries might be car dealerships or computer resellers — they have sales forces, many are closely held, some have had to restructure, for some maybe profit margins have taken a beating because of regulations or changed consumer behavior.

Betsy could find the appropriate trade associations listed in the phone book; in the *Encyclopedia of Associations,* published by Gale Research, which is in the public library; she could ask someone in the business; or she could use her computer to search databases for the trade associations of and articles about the industry.

Personal Marketing to Betsy's Individual Clients

To look for more individuals who might need representation concerning employment contracts *or* severance packages (they are related), we go back to clients Betsy has already represented. Past clients who have been downsized out of corporations probably know of others in their industry. Keeping in touch with them through newsletters or holding a seminar on a related topic, such as negotiating your way into a new job, or what to look for in an employment contract (and asking clients to bring a friend or colleague), would spur referrals.

Secondarily, with the number of industries going through consolidation and other structural changes, writing an article in an industry journal, or holding a public seminar in an easily accessible place, would probably draw an audience of prospects. On the other hand, if the office equipment dealers are downsizing, and as a result want to limit the use of outside counsel, perhaps Betsy could assist owners in protecting themselves from litigation by holding an executive briefing on the topic.

Types of Personal Marketing Tactics

Personal marketing activities include any marketing tactics that you use to meet and communicate with appropriate target audiences or prospective clients. Firm marketing tactics, like exceptions to the rule against hearsay, are *substitutions* for your personal involvement. Here is a list that separates the two:

Personal Marketing	Firm Marketing
Networking	Brochure
Personal selling	Advertising
Client briefing	Public relations
Speaking engagement	
Publish an article	
Newsletter	

Note that all the personal activities are just that — they showcase you, whether in the flesh or in written representation. Personal marketing tactics are the most effective way to market because they put you in position to personally display your competence and build relationships, which is exactly why your best clients choose you.

Networking: The Largest Rolodex Wins!

Personal marketing in the form of networking is the highest payoff strategy because, as in any human enterprise, success is founded on human interrelationships. Or, as a successful friend of mine states, "It's *who* you know first, and *what* you know also." Anytime you get together with other people who might be client prospects, or conduits to other prospective clients, you have set the stage to increase your marketing success. And the most effective contacts come through your Level One clients. How is this done?

Network with He or She Who Must be Obeyed

Peruse your list of Level One clients. These clients produce your paycheck. They buy an intangible product from you — be it advice, a plan, or freedom from anxiety or uncertainty. They probably chose you because they thought they could work well with you, for a variety of interpersonal reasons that predicted success in their minds, and you delivered services that met or exceeded their expectations. Otherwise they would not presently be Level Ones. As I've stressed, this set of clients is the most important marketing segment in your practice; and because of this, you should regularly schedule interactions with them aside and apart from the exact legal matters you've handled for them. Those expandable Level Two clients that you have selected should also be included in your efforts.

What types of activities are appropriate? Social, educational, recreational, legal programs, but outside of your primary nexus, and other activities that add a new layer of interpersonal quality to the working relationship.

Personal Marketing Actions with Level One Clients and Targeted Level Two Clients

Social, Professional, Recreational: Consider combinations of you and clients — sharing a meal, a golf game, or other social event. Mix compatible clients so they get to know one another; mix clients with prospective clients; mix your clients with your network of friends; ask to accompany your client to their favorite network, trade, or professional association — this is a roomful of prospects, and it allows you to learn about industry issues. (More about this "forward" networking in subsequent sections.)

Educational: Briefings, seminars, newsletters that you provide, or that you know about which will benefit your client, are worthwhile ways to enhance your value to your best clients. A briefing or seminar can be as informal as meeting over a cup of coffee. If you run a briefing for some clients, encourage them to bring along a colleague since this will probably be another like-minded individual who may, therefore, be a strong prospect. Consider, too, that the topic does not have to be closely tied to the services you provide. If you have a client who is a tennis fanatic, and you know that the tennis pro at your club is running a workshop on doubles net strategy, think about inviting the client to the workshop.

Forward Networking: Each of your Level One clients has a business and personal network that contains individuals and entities who are just like them, and those analogues and clones are very apt to be great prospects. Let's go back to Betsy and her Level One equipment dealers. The dealers have a regional association that convenes periodically to discuss industry issues, brainstorm problem areas, and socialize. Additionally, they probably attend the yearly nationwide convention of dealers for the same reasons.

Betsy, just like you, should consider asking to accompany one of her clients to a meeting for the valid reason of learning more about the industry and meeting other players — they may have novel approaches to running their businesses, as well as be very qualified prospects for Betsy. Second, as suggested before, Betsy is qualified to be a speaker to this group. She has specific expertise in this industry and, either informally or formally, she can share that expertise through a seminar/workshop/briefing or by writing for the association newsletter or magazine. Depending on personal preference, either means is valuable, but the face-to-face exposure is patently more effective. The same opportunities exist at the national level for the yearly convention. What about Betsy's individual clients? They, too, have affiliations in their industries and communities that present both formal and informal networking opportunities.

The important aspect of forward networking is that you are enmeshing yourself in the networks of your Level One clients. Unless you get all your work from attorney referrals, do not think of your bar association meetings as primary networking events. While you may get some referrals from other attorneys, you cannot network effectively with competitors.

Networking, then, looks like this:

Networking ——>	Level One clients ——>	Forward networking Level One associations
	• social	• attend meetings
	• educational	• give seminars
	• recreational	• write articles

By defining optimal marketing situations through your Level One clients and their affiliations, you can meet multiple client prospects who have needs similar to your present clients'. With your exposure to such qualified audiences and the marketing intelligence they impart, your marketing time will have a greater payoff, and you will also serve your clients better. You will have added a quality to the personal and professional dimensions of your working relationship, and that can't help but be a plus.

Now, look at your diary. If you don't see at least one occasion a week when you are networking through and with your Level One clients, pick up the phone. To help you out, use the Networking Form below and consider installing a personal information manager software program on your computer to keep you on track. See chapter 6 on using computers to support marketing.

NETWORKING FORM

Your Level One and selected Level Two clients should be contacted for networking purposes on a regular basis, in addition to the exact legal work you do for them. Once listed, schedule the phone calls in your diary and make them consistently, say, one or two a day so that it's easy to do.

Client	**Reason for Contact**	**Call Date**
1. ______________	______________	________
2. ______________	______________	________
3. ______________	______________	________
4. ______________	______________	________
5. ______________	______________	________
6. ______________	______________	________
7. ______________	______________	________
8. ______________	______________	________
9. ______________	______________	________
10. ______________	______________	________
11. ______________	______________	________
12. ______________	______________	________

NB: Track results so that if a client declines, you will remember to vary your approach.

Personal Selling

The last step in the marketing cycle is selling. This step requires the same persuasive skills that you might use in the courtroom to negotiate a settlement or convince a judge or jury to consider the merits of your point of view. Although personal selling lacks the adversarial content of these legal interactions, it is still in all a persuasion process. No matter what the challenge or opportunity, your prospects for success are much higher when you pay as much attention to persuasion in all situations, friendly and adversarial, particularly if the stakes are high.

Planning Requirements for Successful Selling

The process of persuasion in personal selling has two phases: rapport building, and the articulation of benefits that meet the listeners' needs. In marketing, the quicker and more easily you establish rapport with prospective clients, the faster they will have enough confidence in your competence, and therefore the more likely they are to choose to work with you. I call the second part of the selling process "Answering the Three Questions," or the 3 Qs. These questions are the ones lurking in the mind of any listener you might have to persuade. They are, specifically:

1. **Why should I listen to you?** Your discussion points need to focus on your specific expertise and experiences to get the listener's attention, referrals, or professional recommendations.
2. **What's in it for me?** Listeners want to hear specifically how your services would benefit them.
3. **Why should I decide now?** Whatever decision you are asking for, be it an opportunity to talk further, meet, or get a client to work with you, you must present compelling and logical reasons to move forward in a style that fits the occasion.

The Importance of Rapport Building

Rapport, meaning a relationship or an agreement, is really a process, one that facilitates the creation of a working relationship or which, by its absence, obliterates any chance of working together or reaching agreements. We build rapport unconsciously because we are social beings. But why is rapport important to marketing? You cannot communicate effectively, nor can you build a relationship with a prospect or client, without rapport. Since your clients and prospects can choose from any number of attorneys competent to do the work, excelling at rapport building will make you stand out from the crowd. As I mentioned earlier, clients tell me that until or unless they feel comfortable with you (translated — until rapport exists), they won't select you. On the other hand, the better the rapport you establish, the more information you will learn about the prospective client, and that is a plus both in evaluating whether you can work with the person, and in helping the prospective client define his or her situation. So, rapport plays an important role in getting and keeping good clients.

In her book *Influencing with Integrity*, Genie Z. LaBorde says, "Rapport is like money: it increases in importance when you do not have it, and when you do have it, a lot of opportunities appear" (p. 27).

The persuasion process, although it is not a straight line sequence, looks like this:

Build rapport ——> Answer the 3 Qs ——> Decision

Rapport means building a degree of affinity between and among people that will offset the differences that always exist. Between you and a prospective client, rapport building brings to the foreground what I call the *le cage* (birds of a feather) factors among people. That is, when rapport exists, there remain articulable commonalities or shared understandings even when differences exist. Rapport allows a prospect to visualize working with you. It puts him or her in the same picture frame.

Facilitating Rapport

Building rapport starts by gathering information, asking open questions, displaying a dependable pattern of behavior so that trustworthiness stands out, and minimizing the differences of personal communication style — word choice, pacing and tone, and body language. For example, you have a better chance at building rapport with a fast-paced, quick-speaking client prospect if you pick up the pace of your language just a bit, particularly if you normally speak slowly. I am not suggesting mimicry—just paying attention, subtly mirroring salient communication styles.

On a personal level it's easier to notice when grave differences in communication style impede even minor relationships. Remember the last time you dialed a mail order retailer and got a customer service rep from another part of the country with a decidedly different pace of language? Or got in a taxi in New York City whose driver was newly arrived from a country whose culture and language you didn't know, and you tried to establish just enough rapport to get across town? These are minor instances. When the stakes are higher, paying attention to rapport-building skills is critical.

Rapport building is the first flaming hoop you must pass through in the persuasion process. Without rapport, you will not get what you want; you won't get the prospective client to say yes. Without rapport, you have no ability to get to know the person standing next to you at a reception. Rapport is the bridge between people that allows for communication and, later, a working relationship.

Building Rapport while Networking

When you are in a roomful of people you don't know, asking open questions will get you information and start conversations. Many people, myself included, are nauseated by the thought of entering a room full of strangers. Open questions get you past the doorway, into conversation, to establish rapport, then on to make acquaintances.

If you prepare your list of open questions beforehand, you won't be caught hanging out in a corner, nibbling on your *hors d'oeuvres* all by your lonesome. Here are some open questions that move conversation and rapport along:

- Who are you?
- What do you do?
- What's important in your work life? Goals?
- What do you do outside of work?
- What's the next step in your career?
- Do you find these meetings helpful? Informative?

Harvey Mackey, master marketer and writer, talks about the value of knowing more about your prospects and clients than any other competitor. His "Mackey 66" survey is a veritable inventory of customer information. His *Sharkware* software program may be a worthwhile information manager for you. Susan RoAne has an audiotape program entitled "How to Work a Room," which may help you build confidence in establishing rapport in those rooms full of strangers.

Building on Rapport

If you encounter someone you'd like to get to know better, exchange cards while mentioning a justifiable reason to meet further. Then mark the back of his or her business card, and call the next day while you're still remembered. If, during the discussion, you've promised to send out some information, do it the next day. Time is your enemy in moving forward with new acquaintances.

The Physical Aspects of Rapport Building

Understanding the physical attributes of establishing rapport is critical; rapport happens through language use, and it also happens through how we appear and move. You can speed the process by emphasizing the *le cage* factors that are physical in nature: matching body position or posture, matching the tone and tempo and word choice of your speech with that of your listener, matching movement rhythms. Again, I am not suggesting that you mirror *exactly* the person with whom you are attempting to establish rapport. Nor am I implying that you can't market into very diverse or different target audiences. I am suggesting that when you accentuate even minor commonalities in communication style with another person, you open the door to affinity — to rapport, in other words — and perhaps then to a working relationship.

The Consultation

Let's move the process ahead to your meeting with a prospective client in your office. Let's hypothesize that you met this person originally as a friend of a client at some group function.

When you bring him or her into your office or conference room, position yourself parallel to your prospective client — on the same side of the desk or conference table. Rapport happens faster side by side. Some attorneys have told me that they don't feel comfortable with this arrangement. I have suggested that they use a low table, like a coffee table or an end table, between themselves and the prospective client. The issue is to remove the desk as a barrier and condition the room for communication.

Ask open questions, not only about the matter at hand but also about the person generally, so that you have a broader picture of this prospective client. Until and unless you have this more detailed portrait, you will not be able to answer the 3 Qs persuasively. Aside from evaluating the legal matter and how or whether it fits with your competency, the "sale" won't be made unless you answer the 3 Qs for the client.

Oftentimes we assume that once a prospective client is in our office for the first consultation, legal information should be the primary or sole focus. When I interview clients, they tell me that they decide whether or not to become a client based on the interpersonal characteristics of the relationship established during the consultation. As a result, however technically expert they feel you are, unless they also feel "comfortable" with you, they will not choose to work with you. So rapport must step in.

Clients also tell me that they want hard information about prices during that first consultation. The reasons for this are twofold. First, they are too anxious to listen before knowing the financial "definition" of the relationship. Anxious people are not good communicators, and *you* need good information from them during this consultation. Second, the clarity with which you explain pricing, terms, and potential costs bespeaks your competence. As more than one client has related to me, "If they (attorneys) can't give reasonable cost estimates, I don't think they know their business." Another litigation client told me he chose to work with the attorney who was able to lay out a schedule of potential costs so that he could marshal and budget monies for the work.

The clear message out of the mouths of Level Ones is that rapport building, even as it relates to painting a clear and accurate financial picture, counts heavily in the decision-making process. Don't wait to introduce the real cost picture in your engagement letter. The letter should reiterate, not introduce, the real financial story.

Publishing Articles

Getting an article into print in a publication that reaches your target audience is a worthy substitute for face-to-face networking under certain conditions. Writing on a subject relevant to your target market allows you to demonstrate your competence and establish a more public reputation for work in a particular field; and it is far less expensive, and far more persuasive, than advertising. But, like advertising, your best result turns on multiple exposures. If you decide to write and publish, plan your work as a series so that when you've successfully delivered your first article, you can pitch the next topic as a suitable follow-up.

Write for Your Target Market

Unless you get all of your clients as referrals from other attorneys, publishing in legal periodicals does not enhance your business development efforts. The questions of what and where to publish will again be answered by your best clients. Your Level Ones, as individuals or as members of a trade, profession or industry, read certain periodicals. If you've done your job establishing rapport and building a good working relationship, you should have some idea about which periodicals might be viable communication vehicles. As a baseline, most people read community newspapers to find out the local scuttlebutt and catch up on gossip. Here are some other ways of choosing publications:

Individual Reading

- Community newspaper
- Magazines
- Affiliation-based periodicals, e.g., religious, social, athletic, political, hobby, recreational

Work Related

- Trade journal
- Newsletters
- Association publications

You can locate any publication in a directory of print and broadcast media such as *The Gale Directory of Publications and Broadcast Media* (in your local library) by geography, subject matter, or specialty. This type of directory (among others) will not, however, tell you all the specific association publications, magazines, newsletters, or bulletins. You must go to the *Encyclopedia of Associations*, published by Gale, to find out whether a client's association has a publication. The encyclopedia will give you national and regional contacts, such as the executive director; a description of the organization; and any publications and meetings. You will need to further localize the contact levels if you want specific exposure. For example, if some of your Level Ones are veterinarians, you will find multiple, general, and specialty veterinary associations with a variety of publications. But if your target market is geographically defined, don't forget to check your local phone book for the local chapter — county or regional — of the veterinary society.

Select a Good Topic

Consider the questions or presenting issues your Level Ones discuss when they first meet with you and in subsequent consultations. These are great subjects to write about; they pique the preexisting interest level of the reader by addressing top-line needs, and they let you develop and communicate information that creates a natural segue to calling you for a consultation. Although you may think these presenting issue topics are too vague, nonsubstantive, or uninteresting, the individual client-buyer usually seeks legal advice when fate has defined need by necessity. The purpose for writing is to create needs by anticipating fate. This womb-to-tomb approach suggests topics such as:

- Why new parents need estate planning; or how to help elderly parents plan for long-term care
- Five reasons to consider bankruptcy; how to restructure loans with creditors
- What to do if you're contemplating divorce
- How to deal with discrimination in the workplace

There are few good sources of consumer information about when to contact a lawyer, what to look for in counsel, or how an attorney can help you in certain situations. Writing articles that address substance, as well as these attorney selection questions, is worthwhile.

On the other hand, Level Ones who represent businesses and other entities have informational needs that are shaped by changes in their industries or marketplaces. Your knowledge of your clients' professional landscape will define a number of worthy topics.

In either case, if you have analytically defined your clients' need for information, and you've selected the publication that reaches them, the pitch to the editor should focus on the convergence of need and readership, as long as the topic(s) have not previously been published. In anticipation of this discussion, call the publication and have them fax or mail an article index to you as well as copies of the publication. Before you call the editor, you must be familiar with the publication. Now, *semper paratus*, dial up your editor.

Contact the Editor

The heart of your conversation with the editor should be planned by you to answer the 3 Qs:

Why should I listen to you? Mr. Editor, your readers and my clients are the same, and they have a growing need for information (describe) about this topic. My work as an attorney focuses on this area.

What's in it for me? Readership and interest in your publication — dollars, in other words.

Why decide now? The topic is timely, of interest, or has not been treated yet by you or your competitive publications.

If you get past these hurdles, you then need to negotiate timetables, deadlines, format (hard copy, diskette, software) and length. Meet your deadline.

Writing for Non-Lawyers

A note about style: Consider your audience and write to be understood. A good friend of mine who is a professional writer and very successful (i.e., one of the most published writers on the editorial page of the *Wall Street Journal*) once told me that the key to getting people to actually read your article is to communicate all salient points in the first paragraph. Then explain the points in the rest of the article. Since your work is worthless if not read, you must grab the reader's interest right off the bat, list the points, say why they're important to the reader, and then develop them. Use examples and stories to keep your audience with you. Use your speaking voice, not your legal writing style, to write for non-legal audiences; and above all, don't use legalisms.

You can test to ensure you are using your speaking voice in two ways. First, read the article out loud to non-lawyers. Do they grasp the information without tons of questions? If they do, assume your material is clearly written. Second, give the article draft to some Level One clients who are part of the target audience. Solicit their feedback and look for ways that you can include them in your writing. They may have real-life stories or quotes you can use; and, it will solidly reinforce your relationship.

Speaking Engagements

For many attorneys, arranging for speaking engagements or being part of a panel discussion is an easy extension of their advocacy skills. But for some practitioners, the mere thought of a speaking engagement ranks right up there with an IRS audit as an ever-to-be-avoided occurrence. Unless you feel your business development future depends on public speaking, you can substitute other communication devices such as article writing and consistent networking.

The beauty of speaking engagements, though, is that your presence makes the persuasiveness of the communication stronger. In addition to the stage time, audience members have a chance to approach you individually afterwards to discuss their issues and concerns. If you have prepared notes or an outline of your remarks (on your letterhead), you also have a nice tangible reminder to leave with the audience.

Selecting a Forum and Getting Scheduled

This is the same basic process we discussed in the article publication section. There are two major differences: First, instead of negotiating with an editor, you will be speaking with an executive director, president, or program chairperson. Second, timing is important. If you are dealing with an *elected* officer of an organization, talking to an outgoing official will only double your work. Since June is most often election month, your best contact time is late summer or early fall. You can research when a national organization has its periodic convention(s) in the *Encyclopedia of Associations,* mentioned earlier.

The fastest means to getting a speaking slot is to have an existing Level One client recommend you. Without belaboring the topic, enmeshing yourself in your clients' networks opens this doorway to you in ways that your own promotional efforts cannot.

With the exceptions noted above, follow the outline for getting published:

1. Match Level One clients' needs for information with the appropriate forum. If there is an industry association or professional group, contact them first.
2. Contact the officer charged with programming, and answer the 3 Qs (Why listen? What's in it for me? Why decide now?). Better yet, have a present client recommend you.
3. Do more than what you promised.

Getting Good at Public Speaking

Public speaking skills are learned usually by repetitive instances of sweaty palms and stomach butterflies. You remember your first time in court? Same deal. Start with the smaller occasions, practice your talk, and move on to bigger fish. Rigorous preparation will make the occasion work for you.

Preparation

Before you embark on your oratorical career, consider *over*-preparation. Reading about the subject of public speaking alone, which I do suggest, is not enough. Good public speakers inform *and* entertain lest the audience sleep, and an audience *will* without entertainment in the form of stories, humor, and personal glimpses. People remember stories, not facts (like your ability to recite nursery rhymes). In contrast, factual data alone is hard to remember — similar to your having to look up that pesky section of an oft-cited statute. Stories make facts memorable.

For most public speakers, the inform part of the equation is not difficult. The entertainment side . . . well, it takes practice and far more planning than the substance.

Skilled speakers, actors, entertainers, and litigators have the ability to sit in witness of their own presentation (to read the reactions of the audience, in other words) and to adjust their technique to the audience. This is not manipulative—it is a studied and respectful meditation on the construction of the rapport bridge which, between speaker and audience, spans a wide chasm indeed. Once you've fallen into that void in a speaking engagement, you will want to study more about bridges.

Rigorous preparation and realistic rehearsals give you the mental control to read and adjust to the audience. Without preparation, even minor adjustments will throw off your presentation and make you appear unprofessional. One somnolent person in an audience of 500 can be distraction enough to make you forget your speech. That cart of dishes that just clattered down the hotel hall can make the ill-prepared speaker appear to have short-term memory deficits.

There are many good books that can help you in preparation, some of which are listed in the bibliography of this book. A few that I rely on are:

1. *The American Speaker, Your Guide to Successful Speaking,* by Aram Bakshian, Jr., editor, Georgetown Publishing House, 1994.
2. *The Overnight Guide to Public Speaking,* by Ed Wohlmuth, published by Penguin, USA, in paperback.
3. *I'd Rather Die Than Give a Speech,* by Michael Klepper, Irwin Professional Publishing, 1994.

Tips and Traps:

1. Lay out salient issues, starting with an exposition of main points, just like an article. After previewing your points, reintroduce each one as you get to it — major idea first, then digress. Connect the major points so the talk flows and holds together.
2. Wrap stories, vignettes, and humor around the major issues. Make sure these illuminate and amplify the facts so that they are memorable.
3. As you transition from point to point, make *very* explicit how the pieces interrelate. Your knowledge of the subject matter allows you to mentally skip over or delete these relationship bridges. But your audience requires these connectors; they're not the experts. You can lose your audience with this seemingly elliptical speech. They'll perceive it as poor communication on your part, and they will stop paying attention and start chatting.
4. Recap the major points; go over why they were important, and tell the audience what they should do as a result of getting this information, for example, ". . . and if you think that any of these issues or facts may be important to you, you should talk to a lawyer." That's an obvious outtake. Subtlety works just as well, but do give follow-up instructions.
5. Practice your talk as much as you can in front of colleagues whose judgment you trust — and a mirror, your family, a video camera, pets, etc. Record these happy rehearsals on videotape or audiotape. Remove yourself to a sequestered place and then review them multiple times. First time around don't take notes; just pretend you are the audience. Have other people (non-lawyers, if that is your audience, or helpful clients) look or listen to the tapes to give you feedback. Don't stint on this stage of your preparation — this is your safety net.
6. Each time you practice, exorcise those annoying physical habits and edit out the speech fillers like "uhh" and "um," "okay" and terms of art. Note and change these habits: looking in only one direction, overly repetitive gestures, too rapid speech or nodding assent to your

own suggestions. These personal quirks have a far more powerful impact than the substance of your message, and they will cloud the message.

7. Never allow yourself to be scheduled to deliver your talk directly after a meal or at the tail end of a program. Your audience will be asleep or trying to sneak out unless, of course, your sparkling personality or international fame obviate these natural conditions. In an earlier life, I allowed myself to be scheduled into the double-whammy slot, that is, after lunch and the last speaker of a conference. When I shortened my remarks, because the audience members were visibly chafing to leave, they were thankful; not so the conference chairperson — who, by the way, also paid out the honoraria, which had to be renegotiated.

Delivery

1. Write out and send your personal introduction to whomever will do the honors at the event. Never rely on the imputed perspicacity and linguistic insight of the introducer to put this together. In particular, if you have a hard-to-pronounce name like Filip — pronounced correctly "Phillip," but most often "Fileep" — be overly helpful. Make sure the audiovisual equipment you have requested has in fact been ordered. (Visual material will help your speech.) Check to make sure that any written material accompanying your talk will be distributed appropriately. (Include an outline of your remarks, your brochure, and any article reprints that add to your speech.)
2. Arrive before anyone else, and check out the room and the audiovisual equipment. Note how the audience will be seated *vis-a-vis* the podium. Stand in the back of the room and view the podium: Is it easy to see, are there obstacles that can be moved? If you are using an overhead projector, slide projector, or TV monitor, make sure it can be seen easily. Use the media and check for clarity. When your inspection is done to your satisfaction, find somewhere quiet to sit down, relax yourself (sans alcohol), and visualize a successful speech. Relax your face, slow your breathing, and be yourself.
3. When you start, tell the audience important *attention-getting facts*, to wit:
   - You're expert at this topic
   - You will not be long-winded or boring
   - The material is important
   - You will leave time for questions
4. Now, deliver as you have prepared.

What kinds of results should you get from this type of activity? More than likely, a small number of immediately interested parties. Others will call you months later, but these prospects, even though slow in coming, represent a well-qualified future; they know your expertise and thus have solid reasons to call you, and are probably about to make a buying decision. As a result, such well-qualified prospects have a high loyalty rate.

In addition to shorter and longer term prospective clients, you will immediately reap many new connections and referral sources within the target audience, some inquiries, and a few real new clients who are just like your Level Ones. If you can get the attendance list (always ask for it), the names ought to be added to your marketing database for newsletters, invitations to client functions, or reprints of articles you've published.

Client Functions and Communiqués

On any given day in your practice you probably read or hear about events, litigation, changes in the law or in regulations, or other news that causes you to think about communicating with your clients. Typically, though, there's just not enough time to pick up the phone or write a letter. However, you shouldn't miss this opportunity to expand your preventative and consultative role. Level One clients tell me they want more of this type of proactive interaction, and they *value* advisors who take the time to bring them information they can use.

Running meetings, or sending out some other communication, such as a newsletter, can efficiently manage the time constraints of your practice. With the plethora of "advisors" out in the marketplace reaching your clients, your initiative, however informal, can position you as the most important advisor, *primus inter pares* (first among equals). Let's look at how this can work for you, even with your busy schedule.

He and She Who Must Be Obeyed: Communication

The client retention process as a genre of marketing is, in its most elemental form, an interactive communication process between attorney and important client groups. This is not so different from the growth and maintenance of any other human relationship, except that the boundaries are different. Any good working relationship depends on gaining and exchanging information, soliciting feedback, and enlarging the value of the relationship to both parties.

In looking at the maintenance of a working relationship, the timeliness and quality of the interactions are critical. Consider asking your best clients to specify the types of subjects they might need to learn about, and use their ideas to set up briefings on a quarterly or semi-annual basis. You can do this with a short written questionnaire sent out with the invoices. (Check the examples at the end of this chapter.)

Client Functions

Client functions, be they informal conversations or more structured affairs such as social gatherings, briefings, or workshops, or written substitutes like newsletters, are just such interactions that support growth in the scope and quality of your working relationship. They allow your clients to think of you once again as an advisor. They allow you to encourage your best clients to bring colleagues with them to increase referrals, and they allow you to expand the menu of services you put before your Level Ones.

A Short Seminar Success Story

A five-member firm that practices labor and employment law representing unions and individuals in the workplace decided to hold a labor law seminar for shop stewards and union officials. They had not held a seminar in six years, and they worried at the outset of planning that the expense-to-payback ratio would not make it worthwhile. They went ahead and invitations in the form of a letter were sent to 250 union officials. The letters were followed up by phone calls by an administrative assistant to facilitate registration and answer questions such as "Can I bring a colleague?" (Of course.) The letter could also be faxed back for registration.

Over 100 people signed up for the three-hour seminar, which was followed by a two-hour reception at which some 120 officials and friends talked, networked, and shared information. On the evaluation form (see the Seminar Evaluation Form at the end of this chapter), almost all the attendees asked for information on other firm services and for more seminars, and two new non-client unions asked for the attorneys to meet with them. A follow-up thank-you letter was sent to each attendee listing the specific attorneys who handled different practice areas.

Needless to say, the law firm was pleased.

The Recipe for Seminar/Meeting Success

1. Query your client base for topic suggestions and build your agenda with this advice. (See survey forms at the end of this chapter.)
2. Contact hotels or other meeting places to arrange for a meeting room, catering, and audiovisual equipment. Go see the hotels you are interested in and specifically visit the room you are planning to use *while it is in use.* Make sure that the room does not adjoin noisy hotel areas such as the kitchen; running a meeting with the clatter of dishes in the background is very distracting.

   Arrange for a registration table outside of the meeting room. Have name tags, tent cards, and a registration sign-in log at the table. Your written materials should be set out on the meeting room tables in front of each seat. Decide how you want the room and tables set up.
3. Four to six weeks beforehand, send out invitations (with directions to the hotel and its phone number) that include a stamped, self-addressed envelope. Make the registration part of the one-page letter. Specifically mention that attendees can bring friends or colleagues. Put your fax number on it and also tell registrants that they can fax back the letter to register.
4. One week prior to the event, call each invitee to firm up attendance and answer any questions. Even though some will have already responded, they may have questions (Can I bring a colleague? etc.) and you literally want to *shepherd* them into the meeting. Too many attendees can be dealt with, but too few make for a disaster.
5. Seminar materials should include information on the substance of the meeting, your firm brochure or a one-page description of your firm or practice, your business card, and an evaluation form.
6. The day of the event, arrive at *least* two hours early to check on setup, lobby notices, and door signs, and the audiovisual equipment. Locate your sales or catering manager *and* the general manager of the hotel and get their phone numbers so that you can call them quickly if necessary.
7. At the end of your meeting, have the attendees fill out the evaluation forms. Ask for honest responses and genuine feedback, and collect the forms.
8. Send out a thank-you letter immediately. Discuss any future follow-up actions, and be responsive to the feedback you received. Specifically, if you have received requests for meetings, or if you have received any negative evaluations, call those respondents *immediately.*

Even if you run a small meeting in your office for your best clients, the result of this type of activity supports your long-term relationship with your clients and their invited guests. Always allow for guest colleagues to attend, since they will share similar needs. Your meeting is a great opportunity to get to know new potential clients in a consultative atmosphere.

Similarly, you can hold informal briefings over a cup of coffee, over a meal, via a telephone conference call, or through a letter or newsletter. If your format is written, make sure that you include a fax-back or mail-back response portion that allows the receiver to ask for further information. The outcome of this sort of client function or communication can be new matters, referrals, and additional work from your present clients. These events build loyalty and stop client defections, too.

Written Communiqués

Check the pile of mail on your desk. Chances are there are at least a few "newsletters" in the stack. You probably dispose of many of them without reading them. The same is true for each of your clients. Although most of these communiqués get tossed into the round file, the important issue is that *your* expertise is competing for your clients' attention. If you choose to send out a newsletter to keep your clients informed, there are some guidelines that can make your "newsletter" stand out and get read.

How to Invite Readership

1. Send your newsletter out on your letterhead; letters from attorneys will at least get opened. Print your envelopes rather than using labels, if possible. Print the appropriate disclaimer at the bottom of the newsletter stating, "This is not legal advice. . . ." Indeed, what you are doing is sending an *alert*, not advice.
2. Keep the substance short and topical — one page with topics underscored, bulleted, or boldfaced for ease of perusal. You are not giving advice, but merely alerting your clients. Also, busy non-lawyers won't read beyond scanning the document, so you must pull them into the text visually.
3. Let the reader know what he or she can do to get more information: call your office, schedule an appointment, sign up for a briefing you may have scheduled on the subject, receive a reprint of an article you've written, etc. If your clients have faxes, you may want to include a fax-back response portion on the bottom of the letter. If you do this, put your fax number in bold right at the response portion.
4. When you get responses, ensure that you get back to the client quickly. If the reader asks for a callback, make sure you or your assistant asks for a particular time to call. Your opportunity to enlarge the working relationship will fade with time passed.

A Short Story about Newsletters

A solo practitioner who does criminal and white-collar defense work noticed a Supreme Court decision *(Ratzlaf v. U.S.,* 1994 WL 4189 (U.S.) that had import for individuals and business owners. The decision — at least temporarily — impeded the Justice Department's ability to prove money laundering cases: ". . . the Government must prove that the defendant acted with knowledge that the structuring he or she undertook was unlawful, not simply that the defendant's purpose was to circumvent a bank's reporting obligation." While the decision was reported in the press, there were non-clients, such as trade associations, whose members handled a lot of cash, who were unaware of the decision and its potential ramifications for them. Some phone calls to these trade organizations proved that they were very interested in informing their members about this decision. A two-page "white paper" from the attorney was sent to the requesting organizations; it was sent out to the associations' members with the attorney's name, address, and phone number listed.

Not a bad target audience.

Time Management for the Harried

My first manager in the corporate world used to intone, "Plan your work, work your plan." Easy for him to say; he had a supporting cast of thousands, and I had my own devices — long hours, demanding clients, and a large bottle of aspirin to keep headaches at bay.

Given our discussion thus far, the thought may have crossed your mind: "I have no time to do this stuff — I have client work to do!" All right, let's simplify. Louis Pasteur said something about chance only favoring the prepared mind. The Marketing Action Plan on subsequent pages is just such a planning device to efficiently move you from worry to action. It brings us full circle from planning strategy to plotting out a calendar that keeps you on track and minimizes your time commitments.

In using the Plan, the important outcome is that you have a monthly and yearly calendar of business development tactics that move you toward your marketing goals. Here is a list of guidelines for those calendars that I have found quantifies marketing tactics into eminently doable chunks:

Twelve-Month Calendar

- one client function each quarter, be it a newsletter or briefing
- one or two social events for clients
- holiday cards if you send them
- one published article; send reprints to appropriate clients and your network
- one or two speaking engagements
- one client survey

Monthly Calendar

- attend a networking event each week — an association meeting with a client, a community event, or social event
- two to three meals with important clients
- "news" letters to clients as necessary
- press releases or announcements as needed — changes in address, upcoming speaking engagements, releases to the media for important litigation, etc.
- use the Month End Evaluator to review your results for their financial impact

Weekly Calendar

- events and engagements as scheduled above
- five to ten phone calls to follow up on networking contacts soon after the event; schedule time to do two calls a day, one early and one late, and you will get this task done.
- at the end of each week, review your progress

The purpose of this Marketing Action Plan is to consistently execute your marketing tactics in a minimum amount of time, leaving you free to practice law. It is a subset of a firm marketing plan, or an individual substitute if none exists. Consistent actions aimed at your Level Ones and their analogues will produce results you want. While the initiation of these activities may be new and therefore burdensome, the time commitments diminish dramatically after the first pass.

In chapter 3, we will add tactics that develop your firm's image — brochures, press releases, and the like. However, the personal marketing tactics discussed in this chapter give you the quickest results because they are active, interpersonal, and put you in greater contact with clients and prospects.

MARKETING ACTION PLAN

A tactical marketing planner for individuals, practice groups, departments, or firms.

This marketing action plan has four parts:

1. Marketing Strategy and Goals
2. Twelve-Month Tactical Calendar
3. Month End Evaluator
4. Associations and Publications/Media

How to Use This Plan

- Read through the plan so that you are familiar with its parts. This plan is designed to translate your marketing or practice development goals into a 12-month calendar of tactics. Each month's tactics should be selected to produce gains in profitability and the absolute size of your practice.
- Flip to Section 2 and pull this month's and next month's *tactical calendars*. Start filling in your marketing tactics on this and next month's tactical calendars (Section 2). Put your dates in your diary and/or calendar so that you don't forget to implement these steps.
- Use the **Target Market/Cross-Selling Forms** to list out contacts you may have so that you can get in touch (preferably by phone) and set up a meeting to network, help open doors, get an appointment, learn industry news, etc. Remember that help is traded, not given.
- At the end of each month, use the **Month End Evaluator** in Section 3. You will want to inspect your financial results to see:
  — if marketing expenses are, on average, 3 percent of revenues
  — if your financial gains stem from marketing tactics and which ones; these are tactics to repeat and enhance
  — which non-productive tactics to eliminate
  — if revenues are emanating from new target markets; then expand your reach by finding print and broadcast media, and periodicals which communicate with this new market.

The purpose of this action plan is to put your marketing strategy into action so that your practice grows.

THE STEPS OF GOOD MARKETING

Step One

The results of a well-thought-out marketing plan are positive financial results and enhanced client services. *We can affect the profitability of your practice the most by focusing first on your client retention rate.* That rate incorporates both cross-selling opportunities and getting referrals from your present clients. To enhance your retention rate, we work on increasing the two-way interactions you have with your clients.

Step Two

As a second step, we look to add net new clients by allowing you and your work to stand out and stand apart from your competitors'. That entails increasing your contact level through associations and networks, and providing exposure through some media — as in getting articles written and placed in appropriate periodicals, press releases written, or speaking engagements in front of good audiences.

As a matter of course, you will find some tactics work better than others. For that reason, I have provided you with a *Month End Evaluator.* The Evaluator will help you analyze which tactics led to new business, and which didn't; weed out the unproductive tactics, repeat and enhance the ones which work for you. I call this month-end review managing to deviations, and it is a critical part in managing your efforts so that profitability is augmented.

Over time, you will want to refine your tactics or add new ones. Growing a practice is a continuous, creative process.

Step Three

Keep in mind that even the most negative market forces — too many competitors, low marketing budgets, low-priced competition — can be overcome by the consistent implementation of solid marketing tactics. It is the consistent and refined execution of your tactics that will result in your best gains in both growth and profitability.

MARKETING STRATEGY

A marketing strategy is like a road map through unknown territory; it keeps you on track and looking to what is ahead, and it minimizes mistakes. Most importantly, a marketing strategy provides you with a means of testing your marketing decisions for consistency, so that what you do, and spend money on, is worthwhile and not off the track and wasteful.

It is this "truing up" process that gives your firm competitive advantage. The *Month End Evaluator* helps you analyze results in a way that eliminates unproductive permutations in your marketing strategy.

Competitive advantage, then, springs from

1. consistent, well-reasoned and thoughtful implementation of your marketing strategy, and
2. staking out a market niche, or "position," that communicates and delivers valuable and unique services to your clients. The definition of "unique" is both substantive and procedural. Obviously, the substance of your work is critically important. However, the rapport and relationship (procedural elements) portion is of greater interest to your clients. In sum, how well you establish and maintain the quality of your relationship with a client has a weightier differentiation value than substantive inputs. Substance counts, and it is expected by the client; rapport, however, will make or break the relationship. For more on this, see these article reprints following chapter 4: "Holding on to the Client and to Profitability," *New York Law Journal*, and "What Do Clients Want, Anyhow?," *Brooklyn Barrister*.

Two Types of Strategies

Marketing strategies come in two major flavors: low-cost production and differentiation. Why is it important to *choose* and follow a strategy? Doing so saves your most important finite resources — time and money. By making marketing decisions which are consistent with your strategy, you improve the probability of success.

For example, let's say that your firm had chosen to follow a low-cost production strategy due to high-volume, repetitious matters which could be worked on by lower-salaried associates. In light of that strategy choice, it would make greater financial sense to use profits to open more offices to pump up volume, rather than to spend the same profits publishing a full-color, ten-page brochure.

Marketing strategies defined:

1. Low-cost producer, which seeks primarily to manage the costs of production so that the firm makes good margins based on volume, scale, and cost efficiencies. If your firm does high-volume, repetitive work, this may be your pathway.
2. Differentiation, which derives profit margin production from the successful communication and delivery of unique benefits to a target audience. A premium price is obtained for the "value" of the portrayed and perceived unique services of the firm. When clients say, "I feel comfortable working with you," often they are connoting a host of unique values derived from your substantive work, and, more importantly, the quality of the working relationship among you, the client, and your staff.

Marketing Goals

Marketing goals are broadly stated targets which are to be achieved through marketing operations called tactics.

Goals work best when they are quantifiable. They can affect income or expenses.

Examples:

- add two new litigation clients per quarter
- reduce operating expenses 2 percent per quarter
- increase revenues 8 percent this year
- improve cash flow by reducing days outstanding to 32 days

Because numerous steps or tactics are required to effectuate each goal, limiting the number of goals to two or three per year works best.

The marketing goals for your practice might be:

1. Increase new matters opened, or revenues, by 7 percent over the next 12 months.
2. Institute an aggressive public relations and client function schedule, so that we are doing 10 percent more business at year end.

YOUR MARKETING GOALS:

1. ____
   ____
2. ____
   ____

Twelve-Month Tactical Calendar

When you look behind marketing goals, there are numerous actions or tactics needed to effectuate each goal. For example, to increase revenues this year, many client development activities would be needed, from professional networking to facilitating referrals and beyond.

We array the tactics on a 12-month planner to match market needs with your available time and money resources. From here we move to individual sheets, or monthly tactical calendars, which list your tactics *plus* your revenue and expense forecast.

When we have marked up each month, you will need to transfer the tactics and forecasts to your calendar or diary. Following is a sample monthly tactical calendar, and a blank worksheet is provided on the next page.

SAMPLE TACTICAL CALENDAR

Month: August Revenue forecast: $__________

Expense forecast: $__________

Tactics:

1. Submit article to the American Management Association's *Small Business Reports*, "How to Negotiate a Loan Restructuring."
2. Speaking engagement at the American Banking Association, loan workout committee.
3. Lunch with five Level One clients to apprise them of changes affecting their businesses.

TACTICAL CALENDAR

(fill out at the beginning of month)

MONTH: ____

Revenue forecast: $____________

Expense forecast: $____________

Marketing tactics which will support your goals and stimulate profitable growth:

____

____

____

____

____

____

____

____

____

____

____

____

____

____

____

____

____

____

____

____

____

FORECAST SHEET

(Fill out/update weekly)

CLIENT/ACCOUNT	MATTER/VALUE	CLOSE DATE
1.________		
2.________		
3.________		
4.________		
5.________		
6.________		
7.________		
8.________		
9.________		
10.________		

CROSS-SELLING/TARGET ACCOUNTS

(Fill out monthly)

CLIENT/ACCOUNT MATTER/VALUE TARGET DATE

1.______________________________

2.______________________________

3.______________________________

4.______________________________

5.______________________________

6.______________________________

7.______________________________

8.______________________________

9.______________________________

10.______________________________

MONTH-END EVALUATOR

1. Gross revenues: $_________ Expenses divided by revenues: _________%

   Less marketing expenses: $_________ Net revenue: $_________

2. Trends in revenue? Expenses?
3. Cash flow considerations
4. Are revenues from marketing tactics?
   Yes: Saturate market, find analogues.

   No: Is this a potential new target market?

5. Major revenue sources:

   a.

   b.

   c.

6. Which are best by gross margin percent and total dollars?
   - How can you encourage more of this?
   - Any room to maximize margins?
   - Accounts which should be dropped?

TO DO:

____

____

____

____

____

____

____

____

____

Associations and Publications/Media: Some Samples

(Keep these listings in your database for future reference and use.)

Association Contacts

Ms. Carole Buhl
Association of Retired Americans
PO Box 610286
Dallas, TX 75261

Mr. Edward Carty
Long Island Association
80 Happauge Rd.
Commack, NY 11725
516-499-4400
516-777-3143 (fax#)

Mr. Ronald Combs
International Association of Registered Financial Planners
305 E. Franklin Ave.
El Paso, TX 79901
915-544-7947
800-749-7947 (fax#)

Mr. James Cunningham
NJ Association of Health Care Facilities
2131 Rt. 33
Lexinton Square Commons
Trenton, NJ 08690
609-890-8700
584-1047 (fax#)

Mr. Val Halamandaris
National Association for Home Care
519 C St. NE
Stanton Park
Washington, DC 20002
202-547-7424
202-547-3540 (fax#)

Mr. Clifford Heath
NJ Asphalt Pavement Association
101 Interchange Plaza
Cranbury, NJ 08512
609-655-2030
609-655-2733 (fax#)

Ms. Lee O'Toole
NJ Bankers Association
PO Box 573
Princeton, NJ 08542
609-924-5550
609-924-8441 (fax#)

Ms. Ann Pakalski
Dental Group Management Association
c/o North Point Dental Group
7040 N. Port Washington
Milwaukee, WI 53211
414-224-1020

Mr. Hal Prink
Medical Group Management Association
104 Inverness Terr. E.
Englewood, CA 80112
303-799-1111
303-643-4427 (fax#)

Ms. Margaret Schulte
Healthcare Financial Management Association
Two Westbrook Corporate Center
Ste. 700
Westchester, IL 60154
708-531-9600
708-531-0032 (fax#)

Mr. Michael Smith
Bankers Association of New York State
485 Lexington Ave.
NY, NY 10017
212-949-1155
212-949-1183 (fax#)

Mr. James Stroop
Association of Human Resource Systems Professionals
PO Box 801646
Dallas, TX 75380
214-661-3727
214-386-8180 (fax#)

Mr. Edward Truschke
Alzheimer's Association
70 E. Lake St.
Ste. 600
Chicago, IL 60601
312-853-3060
312-853-3660 (fax#)

Publication/Media Contacts

Editor
American Lawyer
600 Third Ave.
NY, NY 10016
212-973-2800
212-972-6258 (fax#)

Editor
National Law Journal
345 Park Avenue South
New York, NY 10010
212-692-1875

Mr. Steven Adler
Wall Street Journal
200 Liberty St.
NY, NY 10281
212-416-2000
212-416-2653 (fax#)

Ms. Jan Hoffman
New York Times
229 W. 43rd.
NY, NY 10036
212-556-1234

Ms. Jane Bensahel
S. Corps: Jnl. of Tax, Legal, & Business Strategies
Executive Enterprises Publ. Co., Inc.
22 W. 21st St.
NY, NY 10010-6904
212-645-7880
212-645-8689 (fax#)

Mr. Robert Cooper
Fordham Lawyer
Fordham Law School, Rm. 125
140 W. 62nd St.
NY, NY 10023
212-636-6806
212-636-6958 (fax#)

Mr. Greg David
Crains New York Business
220 E. 42nd St.
NY, NY 10017
212-210-0100
212-210-0799 (fax#)

News Director
WSJ Radio Network
200 Liberty St., 14th Fl.
NY, NY 10281
212-416-2381
212-416-4195 (fax#)

News Director
ABC
77 W. 66th St.
NY, NY 10023
212-456-7777

News Director
CBS
51 W. 52nd St.
NY, NY 10019
212-975-4321

News Director
Fox Broadcasting Company
1211 Avenue of the Americas, 3rd Fl.
NY, NY 10036
212-556-2400

News Director
PBS
1790 Broadway
NY, NY 10019
212-708-3000

Fred Graham
Managing Editor
Courtroom Television Network
600 3rd Ave., 2nd Fl.
NY, NY 10016
212-973-2800

News Director
ABC Radio Networks
77 W. 66th St.
NY, NY 10023
212-456-7777

News Director
CBS Radio Networks
51 W. 52nd St.
NY, NY 10019
212-975-4321

News Director
NPR
801 2nd Ave.
NY, NY 10017
212-490-2444

News Director
WNET TV
356 W. 58th St.
NY, NY 10019
212-560-2000

Ms. Kris Fischer
New York Law Journal
New York Law Publishing Company
345 Park Avenue South
NY, NY 10010
212-779-9200
212-696-4287 (fax#)

Ms. Rachelle Garbarine
N.J. Section Writer
New York Times
229 W. 43rd St.
NY, NY 10036
212-556-7195
212-556-7661 (fax#)

Mr. Louis Grasso
Suffolk Life Newspapers
PO Box 167
Riverhead, NY 11901
516-369-0800
516-369-5930 (fax#)

Ms. Lucinda Harper
Labor Notes Writer
Wall Street Journal
200 Liberty St.
NY, NY 10281
212-416-2000
212-416-2653 (fax#)

Mr. John Leventhal
Editor
Brooklyn Bar Journal
16 Court St.
Brooklyn, NY 11241
718-855-2600
718-797-1713 (fax#)

Legal/Business Editor
Bloomberg News Radio
499 Park Ave.
NY, NY 10022
212-318-2300
212-980-2341 (fax#)

Ms. Erica Penzer
American Lawyer
600 Third Ave.
NY, NY 10016
212-973-2800
212-972-6258(fax#)

Ms. Barbara Presley Noble
New York Times
229 W. 43rd. St.
NY, NY 10036

Mr. Paul Townsend
Long Island Business News
2150 Smithtown Ave.
Ronkonkoma, NY 11779
516-737-1700
516-737-1890 (fax#)

Ms. Cathleen Urell
Long Island Business News
2150 Smithtown Rd.
Ronkonkoma, NY 11779
516-737-1700
516-737-1890 (fax#)

Ms. Maureen Wise
Women's League Outlook
48 E. 74th St.
NY, NY 10021
212-628-1600
212-772-3507 (fax#)

SURVEY EXAMPLE

We would appreciate your comments so that we can deliver the best legal services to you. You do *not* have to sign your name. Please return by fax at [fax no.], or in the stamped envelope we have provided.

Circle a number: 1 = Great 2 = OK 3 = Poor

1. How would you rate the overall service you received?	1	2	3
2. Was the attorney responsive to you?	1	2	3
3. Was the staff courteous?	1	2	3
4. If you were to recommend us to a friend, how would you rate us?	1	2	3

5. Can you tell us *anything* that would help us deliver better service to you in the future? ______________________________

____

____

6. We frequently hold briefings in these practice areas. Circle ones to which you would like to be invited (substitute your practice areas):

Employment issues	Bankruptcy
Retirement and pension	Social security
Personal injury	Workers' compensation

Your suggestion: ______________________

Your name (optional):______________________________

Would you like us to call you? Yes_____ No_____

Would you like to receive our newsletter? Yes_____ No_____

QUESTIONNAIRE

I would appreciate your assistance in filling this out so I can be of better service to you this year. Thanks!

Your name: ____

1. Would you like more information on (check as many as you wish):

   ___ Debtor/creditor issues
   ___ Bankruptcy issues
   ___ Business advisement
   ___ A topic I have not mentioned:__________
   ____
   ____
   ___ Real estate
   ___ Personal injury
   ___ Wills and trusts
   ___ Estate and tax planning, including elder law

2. Over the next 12 months, is there a specific time that you wish me to be in contact with you? If so, when?

   Month:____________________

3. A major change in your life like births, death, illness, separation, divorce, marriage, disability, the purchase or sale of a home or business, bankruptcy, or unemployment, are usually appropriate times to check with your attorney. Are any of these changes about to occur in your life? Yes ___ No ___

4. Many times clients wait till the last minute before consulting with their lawyer because they fear the expense. Are you aware that you can call or visit the first time free at my office? Yes ___ No ___

5. Over the next six months I am going to hold seminars which address critical legal issues. What topics would you like me to develop?

   ____

   ____

   ____

   ____

Mail back in the enclosed envelope or fax back to (   )

Chapter Three

Firm-wide Marketing Tactics

INTRODUCTION

IN THE PREVIOUS chapters we have discussed how you as an individual can market yourself through networking, public speaking, writing, and other well-planned interactions that present your professionally competent self in front of fertile target audiences. Those face-to-face interactions and their written substitutes (articles, newsletters) are the most powerful marketing tools you have. However, given the constraints on your time, and the need to market your *firm* to broader target audiences, you should consider additional marketing steps that communicate the collective personality of your firm. These are *brochures, advertising*, and *public relations*.

These less personal, passive marketing techniques are not substitutes for your personal marketing, but they are worthy *supportive* additions. In the final analysis, whether you are marketing to individuals or entities, it is you, not your brochure, that prospective clients choose. As a result, personal marketing steps are the most persuasive, and firm-wide marketing is secondary, although supportive.

BROCHURES

Do you really need a brochure? Lots of attorneys go through life without one, and successfully so. The real issue, I believe, is what a brochure can and should do for you without costing a fortune.

Marketing Expert Air

Legal services are an intangible product. Marketing and selling this "expert air" requires some distinct marketing tactics, and that is where brochures fit in. A brochure is a tangible representation of what you do. It allows prospective clients to get a grip on what you can do for them. A brochure is also a cross-selling device that reminds present Level One clients of other services and practice areas you provide. Good clients frequently switch firms because they don't know of your other practice areas. A brochure provides this more complete menu selection.

In the sense that a brochure makes real what you do by giving it tangible form, and because it is both portable and a substitute for your presence, it is a useful investment even for the solo practitioner. Making your investment pay off, however, requires some critical planning and execution steps.

In interviews that I have done with legal clients, many remarked that brochures often went unread — too many words, too little meaning for the reader. Many clients did not understand or care about the significance of legal credentials such as law review, judicial clerkships, or school attendance.

What most clients want to glean from the brochure is an understanding of what the firm does, how it has assisted clients like themselves, its track record, why the firm is proficient at its work, and what makes it *different*. Most interviewees said they scanned brochures, and did not read them in depth (they're mostly non-lawyers, so assume they do not read critically), and that they were visually interested in graphics, bold headers, and lists set off by bullets, *not* lengthy text.

Finally, client interviews have demonstrated that even present clients should get that newly published brochure, for the cross-selling opportunities it may open. Often when firms publish a brochure, they give it to prospective clients and forget about sending it to their present clients. Clients have often remarked that they had no idea that the firm practiced in areas other than the one the clients had used in particular. Many were surprised at the very existence of a brochure.

Here are some guidelines in creating a brochure that works for you:

1. Profile your audience and craft the message to meet its needs. Ask yourself, who will read this brochure, and what are the presenting questions or issues that they come to me for? Build your copy or manuscript around those needs.
2. Tell the reader why you are different in very specific language — cite work done in the practice area, demonstrate your knowledge of the field, mention articles written, speaking engagements, teaching assignments, associations, or organizations to which you belong, etc. Include standard-setting selection language, that is, what to look for, and how to select a lawyer.
3. Tell the reader what you do for clients in language that captures *benefits*, not features or practice areas. For example, you may write that

you help entrepreneurs start and manage their businesses successfully, instead of "Business Law." Construe the language to show the benefits and value of what you do in terms that the layperson can understand.

4. Have the brochure designed by a professional in a format that is highly visual, using bold print, graphic design and color, bullets, pictures, and illustrations. Test the copy and format on actual clients to get their advice.
5. Choose your final design based on both budget constraints and clarity. Your brochure is your stand-in before your target audience so *you* must feel comfortable with it, and your clients must find it a clear and compelling representation of your work.
6. When you have the brochures printed, send them to your Level One clients along with a note from you. Keep a number of them in your briefcase, put them in your waiting area, hand them out to prospects, and pass them along to people in your own network or at speaking engagements. In other words, use them. Don't save them. If you have other members or associates in your firm, get together with them and cover how to use and distribute your brochure.

Budget Constraints

A note on budgetary considerations is important because money is usually the encumbrance to getting a brochure done. You do not need to spend a fortune on this marketing tool. At the low end of the scale you can use a letter-size sheet of good paper stock with a "Z" fold so you have three panels front and back, two colors, and a professional designer for a very affordable price, say under $2,500 or thereabouts. If you consider cutting back on anything, don't scrimp on the professional design; a good designer makes the copy readable, chooses clear typefaces, and makes the print and design look good on the page. Good design invites readership. If you have a design background, do it yourself if you have time. Otherwise, get some professional help.

As I've suggested, brochures do no good sitting on a shelf. Use them whenever you have the opportunity, but remember also that you are the best marketer for your firm, and you, followed up by a brochure, makes a powerful combination.

ADVERTISING

Advertising is any paid-for marketing communication. Advertising can be found in almost any medium: print, TV, radio, computer networks, billboards, coffee mugs, telephone directories, and refrigerator magnets, to name a few. The goal of advertising is to persuade the reader or listener to *take action*. That means to call you up, file the information, or tell someone else about the ad.

As a subset of the marketing mix, advertising's role has changed dramatically in the last decade as our society and culture have changed. "Fractionalization" has occurred — that is, the recognition of diversity, of changed work patterns and new parties who work — and changes in values have increased the fractions, or variety, of a target audience.

Advertising's effect is undercut by the random life occurrences of your audience. You get results if the message speaks to a person who just (randomly) has the need for your services. As a practical matter, by carefully selecting the target audience, media vehicles and the message, you can minimize the effects of randomness and diversity. For example, advertising your employment practice in a journal reaching members of an industry that is consolidating puts your message in front of a susceptible audience.

Types of Advertising

Advertising can be typed generally into one of three categories:

1. *Institutional ads* that promote the institution or firm and its major values. Think of the Rock of Gibraltar in the Prudential ads, or the running-bull Merrill Lynch brokerage ads. These very tangible icons (rocks and bulls) are helpful intellectual handles for the viewer because they translate intangible services into solid values.

   You can use graphic design, illustration, or photos to do the same thing.
2. *Competitive ads* are those that tout your firm over another, such as "Get Met (Metropolitan Life Insurance, Co.), It Pays." The unsaid message is that other firms don't pay. Since outright comparisons are not feasible, given the number of competitors and ethical considerations, subtly underscoring the unique attributes of your firm works just as well and presents a more professional image.
3. *Reminder ads* remind your audience to use your services again, such as the "Don't leave home without it" American Express ad. In the context of law firm advertising, cross-selling other practice areas reminds the audience members that you are capable of handling more types of legal matters than the one practice area they used. Also, using hypothetical questions reminds the audience members of matters they may want to speak to your firm about: "Has the glass ceiling become a brick wall?" (for an employment litigation firm).

The advertising you create may have elements of all three of these types, but what is most important is to define who your target audience is, and to create a finely tuned message that motivates it to take action.

Advertising Checklist

1. *Define your target audience.* Create a profile by asking who are its members, where do they live/work, what are their values? What usually is the presenting issue(s) that a typical client has when he or she comes to your office? Do this analysis by scrutinizing your Level One client list. What media (print, radio, TV) reach the greatest portion of your target audience?

   Be specific. If your clients come from the community, then the community newspaper might be your best bet. However, if your target market consists of regional bottlers and beverage distributors, or ear, nose, and throat doctors practicing in your state, there is probably a specific periodical that reaches them directly through an association or professional society.
2. *Create a message* that fits, or speaks to, this target audience. Make the message succinct, easy to read, and persuasive so that it motivates the viewer to do something: call for an appointment, call for an article or brochure, call to be put on your seminar list, call to talk to you, *take action.* The underlying purpose of an ad is to create an interaction. Consider the difference between these versions of advertising text for the labor and employment firm example used earlier:
   - We represent managerial employees in their relationships with their employers.
   - **Question:** Does the glass ceiling feel like a brick wall? If it does, consult with the law firm of . . .

   Now, suppose you're a commuter on a bus, train, or in a car and you're skimming through the morning paper. Which ad asks you to read it?
3. Use design assistance to make the print ad look good and read well. If you are using radio or TV, professional production help is invaluable, and often required. Test your ad copy with present clients to discern whether it communicates and persuades; ask for their feedback.
4. *Contact the advertising managers* of the media you've selected and ask for a media kit (and copies of the periodical and audio- or videotapes if you're not familiar with the product) and a rate card for prices. These can be mailed or faxed. If you are not sure which periodicals or broadcast media reach your audience, consult a directory such as *The Gale Directory of Publications and Broadcast Media, Editor & Publisher* or *Gebbie Press.*

When you get the media kit, pay attention to the demographic profiles and readership/viewership statistics: Are they on point with your target audience? Finally, call some present advertisers in similar, non-competing businesses or practices and ask about the responses they've been getting, and how long they have used that medium.

5. *Create a media budget/selection* that best fits your goal to reach your audience. You will want to commit to a schedule that gets you a reliable trial for the ad. Advertising execs use a "Rule of Sevens" — run an ad seven times to gauge its effectiveness. You should recover seven to eight times your investment. Check the ad rates and quantity discounts; somewhere between four and ten trials will give you a chance to evaluate the medium.
6. *Set up a tracking mechanism.* Institutionalize a form that queries each caller about how they came to you and make it part of the client intake process. You then can evaluate the effect your ads have had by the number of respondents. Do not expect immediate results. The audience needs multiple exposures to your ads because the incidents that give rise to calling on you are the random ones in their lives.

Professional Announcements vs. Advertising

Much of the foregoing discussion has centered on advertising in the commercial sense, that is, promotional communication directed at a target audience. Professional announcements differ from this form of commercial advertising in that announcements are usually directed to the legal community or to present clients, and their intent is usually to inform, not to seek immediate changes in behavior.

This distinction is important for two reasons:

1. Frequently, when the topic of advertising is bandied about, some attorneys include the informational announcement in the same category; and they usually express some negativity about advertising, per se, since their announcements produced no new clients. Really, these should not be mixed together since they have different economic impacts. I mention this not for the sake of intellectual puritanism, but to keep our focus on creating financial changes from marketing investments made.
2. Sometimes, however, an attorney or a practice may get all of its clients through referrals from other members of the bar. In that sense, announcements or quasi-advertisements that motivate colleagues to *do* something are truly ads, and you might consider transgressing or expanding the creative boundaries beyond the tombstone format to create persuasive pull in your professional announcements.

When to Consider Advertising

Well-planned and well-executed advertising reaches many more members in your target audience than writing, speaking, client functions, or networking. However, as I have stressed, advertising's persuasive impact is lower than these personal marketing tactics because it is a substitute for you, and you are the product. Yet, advertising's very reach makes it a good adjunct to your personal marketing tactics to reinforce name recognition, to remind the audience of your specific expertise, and to enlarge the menu of services and functions you present to clients and their analogues. All of these goals are supported by well-designed, persuasive ads.

If your typical client is an individual who comes to you for one matter only, advertising support can be very productive *in addition* to your personal marketing tactics. You can create awareness of your practice, and you can also inform of unique attributes — weekend hours, multilingual staff, "We come to you" — or whatever sets you apart.

Additionally, make sure that you are mentioning all of your practice areas even if you think your clients are not likely to come back. Remember the lawyer with the bankruptcy practice I mentioned earlier? When clients work with you on a matter, they tend to categorize you as practicing in that one area only. When the next legal issue comes up in their lives, they go somewhere else. Your advertising copy can help you cross-sell your other practice areas.

Advertising Doesn't Supplant Personal Marketing

For most practices, the use of advertising extends and supports personal marketing efforts. Advertising alone is usually not enough. For instance, an attorney in a small firm doing a lot of workers' comp, with a high percentage of Spanish-speaking clients, placed ads in the local Spanish newspaper hoping to increase his client intake. The ads ran for six months. Nothing happened.

What could have made those ads take effect in that target audience? Here is a list that the attorney might consider. Note that it mixes personal *and* firm-wide tactics; and it would work for a practice with both recurring clients and the one-matter-only individuals who are community or geographically based — typically the most difficult target audience to market to.

1. **Get an article published** in the local paper on a common issue or presenting question your clients have; this is free advertising.
2. **Have a workshop in a public place** on the same subject matter. Location is important, particularly if your target audience is likely to have children in tow. Use libraries, schools, your offices if appropri-

ate, or any place that is accessible and nearby. Give it at a workable time.

3. **Get news coverage** for important decisions, emerging issues, changes in the law, or regulations that affect the interests of your target group.
4. **Consider marketing to tangential referral sources** who have contact with your prospective clients on related matters. For instance, the attorney in the workers' comp example wrote an article for the state's medical society magazine entitled, "How to Get Paid by Workers' Compensation," a heartwarming and well-read topic. He also got himself signed up as a guest lecturer at the local medical college, speaking to residents in occupational medicine on the topic of causation and, of course, compensation. He has a database of the attendees.
5. **Get the promotional message to the site** so you will be visible when needed: telephone message pads for the car, the home or office; those tasteful fridge magnets; the Yellow Pages; a radio ad during drive time.
6. **Look for aggregators** (places where prospective clients aggregate) to enhance your ability to reach your target audience. Common aggregators: churches, civic groups, social events, recreational clubs, trade associations. In the case of one New England attorney, it became apparent that he met most of his clients through his yacht club, where he sailed on weekends. He took a more active role in the governance of the club, and subsequently became its president. His practice is booming.
7. **When a prospective client comes in** for a consultation, always hand him or her more than one business card and your brochure if you have one.

Public Relations

Public relations refers mostly to unpaid-for marketing communications, and is another tool in your promotional strategy. Public relations practice encompasses sending out press releases; sponsoring or underwriting events or programs; sending press kits to editors and producers; any media coverage of you or your firm, including announcements in newspaper or magazine calendars; press conferences; and public service announcements that highlight your involvement.

No firm is too small to consider having an active PR strategy. Indeed, PR can really help small firms and solos at a great price (zero) and can convey the attributes of size and importance normally associated with larger firms. While you may not get quoted in the *New York Times*, getting your name out front in your local town may be just as critical to the growth of your practice. As with any other operating system, the more and varied the operating options you have, the greater the probability of success.

So it is with your practice. A well-executed public relations strategy is another option that can enhance your success.

Getting Started

Events and changes in status should trigger your PR program for the issuance of press releases. These should be sent to print and broadcast media that your Level One clients pay attention to, as well as *your* own journals, such as legal periodicals and your law school alumni magazine.

Events include:
- speaking engagement
- noteworthy case
- good decision
- seminar you are holding
- being honored by a group
- receiving an award
- giving a lecture

Changes in status:
- formation/breakup of a partnership, mergers
- addition of a new practice area
- hiring of partners, associates, interns
- change of address
- becoming a partner, a judge, an arbitrator
- admission to the bar in other jurisdictions
- getting an advanced degree
- becoming certified in a practice area, e.g., certified civil trial attorney

Compile a Media Directory

By using a media directory such as *Editor & Publisher, Gale,* or *Gebbie,* you have ready access to names, addresses, and phone and fax numbers in the event that you want to issue a press release or contact a media person. Having the directory in your database and a hard copy available will allow an assistant to draft a release even if you are out of the office. Fax numbers are obviously important for speeding up communications; post them by your fax machine. If you are sending a fax to a large organization, call to get the fax number of the specific editor or producer you wish to contact.

Subcategories in Your Media Directory

- national newspapers, e.g., *New York Times, Wall Street Journal*
- newspapers in major markets, e.g., *Albany Times Union, Village Voice, Amsterdam News*
- alternative publications, e.g., *Downtown Express*
- magazines, e.g., *People, Time, Sports Illustrated*
- trade, business, general consumer magazines, e.g., *Adweek, Inc., Ms.*
- wire services, syndicates, e.g., Associated Press located at 50 Rockefeller Plaza, New York City; North America Syndicate at 235 E. 45th St., New York City
- national TV news and talk shows, e.g., *CBS Evening News, Sally Jessie Raphael, Larry King Live*
- local TV network affiliates
- radio networks, stations, talk show hosts, e.g., AP Radio, 1010 WINS, Rush Limbaugh
- non-legal professional organizations and their newsletter/publications, e.g., American Management Association, *Management Review,* Long Island Association, *Long Island Magazine*
- bar associations, state and county, e.g., *New York State Bar News,* Suffolk County Bar Association, *Suffolk Lawyer*
- legal newspapers, journals, e.g., *New York Law Journal, National Law Journal, American Lawyer*
- alumni bulletins and magazines, e.g., *Fordham Lawyer*

Press/News Releases

Now comes the fortuitous event or change of circumstance that calls for some sort of press coverage. If you can, plan ahead to give the media some time to cover your story. What do you do?

Call the media. When you do, ask for the editor or writer who covers the particular subject of your event — it could be the legal editor, a business writer, the city desk or the labor editor, for example. Chances are the executive and managing editors are not on the front lines, so calling them serves little purpose. In smaller papers, you will sometimes talk to these people, but you want the attention of the writer or editor on the beat. Smaller papers are often part of a chain of papers that can carry your story to many markets, so don't rue the fact that one of the top papers is not paying attention.

Target the appropriate media vehicle and call; newspaper people can still be reached by phone, whereas radio and television folks by and large cannot. Broadcast media often pull from print media, so start there.

But before you call, prepare yourself by knowing the paper and the writer. Read what he or she has written on important or similar topics. Analyze how your event or item fits, why it is important to the readership, and why it should be covered.

Coverage Options

Here are some coverage options you might negotiate:

1. **Calendar**: List your event in the calendar section, professional announcements, or "Who's News" sections. These sections are very well read.
2. **A column item on your event or subject**: Regular column writers can develop the item you have in a more subjective, detailed manner than the coverage it would otherwise receive.
3. **Question/Answer Interview or Expert Commentator**: If you have grumbled epithets when you've noticed that once again the same attorney was quoted on a particular subject by the same newspaper, only motivation holds you back. Chances are that lawyer took the time to build a working relationship with the writer by paying attention to the writer's work, communicating, and sharing expertise.
4. **Feature Story**: These do happen, and sometimes without your intervention. Your client or subject matter may be noteworthy and the news media pick up on it. This type of full-length, prominent article can make a career. (Often you get photos included.) It is this type of story that sparks the television producers to call you up. As a sidebar, there are numerous ethical considerations to think through that will need your professional attention before the fact. As these events unfold, you are in the tumult of public scrutiny, and preparation will be of paramount importance.
5. **Hold a press conference and get media coverage**: Let the press know in advance that you are going to hold a press conference. For example, you may be filing suit against a state agency in an action that has a large dollar potential and is newsworthy. Again, pay attention to ethical considerations.

With your "pitch" prepared, call morning papers in the late morning, and call afternoon papers in the late afternoon to be sensitive to their deadlines. If you are calling a news wire service (e.g., Associated Press), emphasize the broader, less local nature of the story. Introduce yourself, share your purpose in calling, refer to knowing the writer's work, and be concise. Remember the 3 Qs you must answer: Why listen? What's in it for me? Why decide now? On the phone, you have probably 30 seconds to grab attention, so make sure you've prepared a succinct answer to Why listen?

How to Write a Press/News Release

Alternatively, you can mail or fax press releases. This is appropriate for contacting broadcast media; and if you fax, fax in off-peak hours — nights and weekends, for instance. Writing a release is formulaic. As a result, as long as you craft the substantive portion, an assistant can draft the rest. In addition to substance, consider including a quote (from you) that highlights the importance of, or comments on the larger value of, the material.

For example, a plaintiff's attorney in a sexual assault case against a major resort recently won an appeal allowing him a full jury trial against the third-party corporate defendant. Larger context: recourse of victims, usually women, with absent defendants, and the issue of premises liability with a third-party defendant corporation that had a series of such suits pending. In the quote, the attorney commented on the "devious" legal and corporate maneuvering of the third-party defendant resort owner that had tried to shirk its responsibility to protect its guests, most particularly, women. The press release went out to newspapers, legal periodicals, and other print and media concerned with women's issues.

Tips on writing releases:

1. The top of the release should say "Press Release":

Press Release
Your name or firm
Address

For immediate release (date)	**For more information:**
(if sent ahead of time, put **"Please embargo** until this date")	**Your name, address phone and fax** (home and office)

WHITEACRE LAW FIRM ANNOUNCES MERGER WITH BLACKACRE

Text: Use double spacing and describe who, what, where, when, why, and how. Use short, direct language and quotes whenever possible to keep interest. Remember to write in plain English. Avoid legalisms unless absolutely essential. If multi-page, put "more to follow" on the bottom of page one. The last paragraph should contain information about you and/or the firm. At the end, use the signal "###" to denote the end. If sending to more than one person at an organization, always include cc's.

2. Send, fax, or messenger the release with any photographs. Identify the photo subject on the back. If you do not have one, have a 3-by-5-

inch black-and-white, glossy head shot made of yourself to accompany releases, announcements, and articles you have written.

3. If you are making a *major* announcement such as a merger, the addition of a high-profile attorney, or an important verdict, send the release with accompanying materials in a folder — this is called a "press kit." The accompanying materials may be your firm brochure, article reprints, or a fact sheet.
4. Keep a clipping file of your publicity. You may wish to have some pieces available in your waiting area or office.

Refinements

Getting media and press coverage is a matter of establishing a good working relationship with editors, writers, and producers. This process requires that you pay attention to the following:

- Select the appropriate media and person to contact.
- Be prepared with your pitch, rationale, and ideas.
- Be accessible. If you send a release and don't return the ensuing phone calls quickly, you won't get media coverage.
- Follow up. Meet with the press if asked, and always inquire whether more information is needed after the meeting.
- Say thank you. If you get mentioned, send a note of thanks. Send copies to other media contacts so they know what is being written about you or your firm.
- Pay attention to the ethical considerations that are discussed in chapter 7 of this book.

Chapter Four

The Financial Implications of Marketing Decisions

ONE OF THE primary theses of these marketing chapters is that the outgrowth of marketing investments should be a positive change in the financial status of your practice, in addition to client satisfaction and perceived quality. In fact, the money you spend on business development activities should, in your own mind, be categorized as an "investment." They show up in your financial reports as expenses from an accounting point of view. Yet, some investments have better paybacks than others in terms of scale and timing.

If the net result of marketing is a financial change, the timing issue (and cash flows) may be crucial to your practice. Personal marketing tactics — those that are active, interpersonal marketing functions — have a more immediate effect. Firm-wide marketing tactics, brochures, advertising, and public relations support longer term changes on a wider scale because they touch more of your target audience. To recap:

Personal Marketing Tactics

- Faster results
  - personal selling
  - speaking engagements
  - writing assignments
  - newsletters
  - client functions

Firm-wide Marketing Tactics

- Longer term, more far-reaching effects
  - brochure
  - advertising
  - public relations

Creating a Marketing Plan, Budget, and Forecast

Having a marketing plan on hand is akin to having a road map in unknown geography — you make fewer mistakes and waste less time with a map. You do not need to have an extensive plan like the one I've outlined in chapter 1. However, the most critical part of the marketing plan is the financial map — a planned budget of investments and forecast of results based on your marketing tactics and decisions. These are important management tools, whether you are a solo practitioner or managing partner of a large firm, because they allow for a considered use of your finite resources. They also allow for monthly evaluation: What was our actual result against our forecast? Why did we over- or underachieve our goals?

When you ask those questions with your operational numbers right in front of you, you capture the ability to manage to deviations. That is, you can analyze results from the point of view of causation, and then figure out what to do to accelerate or cure those results. Now, the slippery part of marketing results is that they usually do not occur in the month you implement them. For example, you run a seminar in May, and you pick up two new clients in July as a result. But, if you've been tracking where your clients came from on intake, you can, over time, start to attach causation to results. Whatever works, repeat and embellish. On the other hand, do not repeat tactics that produced no results if you feel they had an adequate trial.

After ongoing months of scrutinizing the results, you get a good sense of the time lapse between tactics and results, so both your comfort level and marketing analysis skills get reinforced. This time lapse is called a *sales cycle*. If you can deduce any generalizations about your sales cycle, all the better. Let's say, for instance, you observe that the sales cycle for one type of client is eight months on average, and for another type of client it takes four weeks. There are two important extrapolations: (1) you can use these averages to prepare or tighten up your revenue forecast; and (2) beyond inspecting how each sales cycle might be shortened (can I apply the short cycle tactics to the longer cycle prospects, can I execute the tactics more efficiently, etc.), the relationship of those two numbers is important because you can offset slowing in the client flow from the eight-month sales cycle by boosting your efforts in marketing to the shorter sales cycle clients.

Getting Started

The fastest way to start the budgeting process is to use a 12-month blank calendar on paper or on your computer. We want to project two specific numbers for each month:

1. **Revenues**: Fees generated from new and recurring client work, including WIP (work in process). Your projected new client fees should *not* be forecasted unless you have done all the selling you need to do and you are *only* waiting for "yes" or "no" from the prospect. This instills a reality check.
2. **Expenses**: I have also called these "investments," but here we revert to accounting terminology. These are expenses attributable to marketing tactics, such as postage, hotel conference rooms, travel and entertainment, printing, etc., that you will incur as a result of your planned marketing tactics. A rough estimate is better than none at all. These include recurring expenses and extraordinary ones, such as the cost of running a seminar at a hotel.

Monthly Analysis

In each month, then, you have two projected numbers: revenues and expenses. Expenses as a percentage of revenues is an important ratio. Many firms use a 3 to 5 percent ratio as a guide for containing marketing expenses, but, as with any rule of thumb, there are exceptions. Three percent of a low number may not support any marketing at all; if you have an extraordinary expense (printing a brochure, running a seminar), it may run much higher —10 to 14 percent. With those considerations in mind, watch the ratio for unaccounted changes, a low percentage that tells you to beef up your efforts, or a high percentage that over time yields poor results. You may want to discontinue the latter.

At the end of each month, compare your budgeted (or forecasted) revenues and expenses to the actual results. The **Month End Evaluator** in the Marketing Action Plan will lead you through the analysis.

Other Financial Indicators to Monitor

Marketing tactics cost and generate money, so there is an expense and revenue impact. Money also has a time shape or speed to it, which is easy to recognize in its slow speed — slow cash flow. Slow cash can debilitate a practice faster than a speeding bullet. Just when you are ready to kick your marketing program into high gear and run a client conference, you realize that collections have been slow and, with no cash on hand, you can't run your program. You can suffer this chicken-and-egg conundrum in hundreds of permutations, and they are all deleterious to your practice.

So how do you monitor and manage cash objectives? One report that you should have your hands on weekly is your accounts receivable report. Receivables are classified in a 30-, 60- or 90-day format, depending on how long the invoiced amount (the receivable) has aged. You should notice the percentage of clients in each category and your average number of days outstanding, or "DSO."

As receivables age, say, as they fall from 60 to 90 days, they become harder to collect. The passage of time slows the wallet. Therefore, slowing shifts in your receivables, and a concomitant rise in your DSO, will make life miserable. How do you better manage cash? Here are some tips:

1. **Choose better clients**. This sounds specious, but cash management does start at the beginning of the marketing cycle. So, keep your Level One clients happy so they come back and refer; and find others like them (chapter 1).
2. **In your first consultation, discuss costs and terms of payment** in very clear terms. Don't be fuzzy. You raise this issue before the client summons up the courage to ask about it. The client will feel better if you take the initiative. This is also the time to *discuss retainers*. Show examples of possible costs and their timing so there are no surprises. In my interviews with Level One clients, they almost unanimously speak of the need for clear cost estimates, given early in the consultation, so that they are less anxious. Information decreases anxiety, even in the face of large estimates.
3. **Bill and collect as quickly as possible.** Putting off your billing slows collections, driving up all of your firm's expenses. If you can collect before the time due, there is a large financial bonus.

Gross Margins

Evaluate incoming clients in terms of expected profit margins and your ability to finance slower paying matters. Besides understanding the absolute size of projected margins, understand that timing plays a role. Many firms that take on contingent work or suffer bad cash flow until judgments or settlements are received then have to use expensive credit lines to pay operational expenses.

As stated before, choosing better clients decreases negative financial impacts. But, there are other considerations:

1. Know the profit margins of the type of work that you do. Your accountant can help you with costing out your work and creating a profit profile of your legal work.
2. Before you take on work, consider alternative billing methods that will keep you from using credit lines or cash reserves to finance the matter. For example, you may wish to create a long-term budget of payments for a litigation client so that he or she knows when to marshal monies for payment.

3. Review profitability each month as you analyze revenues and expenses, bearing in mind that slow payment of receivables is part of the picture. If you are not used to analyzing financial reports, have your accountant assist and teach you so that you become facile with them.
4. Discontinue taking types of clients or matters that have a bad profitability profile. You already have some intuitive feel for what these are. Replace them with better clients through your business development efforts. Cull out any unproductive marketing expenses after a reasonable time.

Here is an example of a profitability evaluation and a list of danger signals that David Politziner, C.P.A. and managing partner of the Flemington, N.J. accounting firm of Amper, Politziner & Mattia, uses. It ties together billing, realization rates, and margins:

	Winning Firms	**Average Firms**	**Your Firm**
Average Billing Rate	$125	$95	
Average Annual Billable Hours per Timekeeper	1,750	1,690	
Annual Realization Rate	.95	.92	
Leverage (Partner-to-Associate Ratio)	1:2.1	1:1	
Margin	48%	38%	
Average Net Income Per Partner	$309,225	$112,256	

Not all of these signals apply to small firms or solo practitioners; some address larger firm issues. But, since you're reading this book, maybe you'll need them in the (near) future.

..... Law Firm Danger Signals .....

1. Are revenues per partner going down?
2. Are revenues per lawyer going down?
3. Is net income per partner going down?
4. Is net income as a percent of gross revenue less than 32 percent?
5. Is partner-to-associate leverage going down?
6. Is turnover going up?
7. Are partner billable hours greater than associate billable hours?
8. Is compensation based on billable hours?

9. Are too many business management tasks handled by a partner rather than delegated to a business manager?
10. Are accounts receivable greater than two and one-half months of revenue?
11. Are more than 25 percent of accounts receivable greater than 75 days old?
12. Is less than 90 percent of WIP (work in process) converted to accounts receivable?
13. Are less than 95 percent of accounts receivable collected?
14. Do accounts receivable and WIP combined amount to more than 70 percent of gross revenues?
15. Is occupancy expense more than 10 percent of net fees?
16. Is debt greater than 50 percent of accounts receivable and WIP combined?
17. Is debt greater than 80 percent of net income?
18. Are associates billing less than 160 hours per month?
19. Are paraprofessionals billing less than 120 hours per month?
20. Are time sheets not turned in within three days?
21. Is only billable time reported, rather than reporting all time, including time devoted to contingency fee cases and firm matters?
22. Are bills normally not mailed until after the 15th of the month?
23. Is the firm not following up within 30 days on unpaid receivables?
24. Are billed client costs significantly less than 9 percent of bills?
25. Is the firm operating without a budget?
26. Is the firm borrowing to pay draws?
27. Does the firm have an expense-reduction culture rather than an expense-control culture?
28. Is the capitalization of the firm less than 30 percent of accrual basis net fees?
29. Is the firm operating without a partnership agreement?
30. Is the firm operating without a formal retirement program?
31. Does the firm have unfunded retirement obligations?
32. Does the firm operate under democratic, committee-run management?
33. Is there insufficient internal communication?
34. Is the firm operating without published criteria for partnership?
35. Is the firm operating without a long-range plan?
36. Is the firm operating without a marketing plan?
37. Do lawyers with the firm display a sole proprietor attitude — that is, is the firm internally competitive rather than externally competitive?

A MAP OF THE MARKETING WORLD

STRATEGIC PLANNING

Define Your Target Market

- Research
- Divide up your base:
  Levels One, Two, Three
  Segments: individuals, entities

Evaluate Your Skills

- Competencies
- Likes/dislikes
- Experience

Ask yourself: What are my resources and disincentives?
What target client needs must I satisfy to be successful?
How do I stack up against my best competitors?

Decide: What strategy, differentiation, or low-cost production will position me for sustainable competitive advantage?
How will I carry it out?

MARKETING MANAGEMENT

STRATEGY SELECTION	—>	SET MARKETING GOALS	—>	SELECT BEST TACTICS
Low-cost Production or Differentiation		2 or 3 goals		Personal vs. Firm-wide
		Marketing Plan • Forecast • Budget		**Marketing Action Plan** With 12-Month Tactical Calendar
REVIEW AS NEEDED		WRITE YEARLY		REVIEW MONTHLY

Reprinted with the permission of the

New York Law Journal

Volume 209-No. 69 New York, Tuesday, April 13, 1993

LAW OFFICE MANAGEMENT

Christine S. Filip

Holding on to the Client and Profitability

The times are too rigorous to forget that client retention is the requisite first phase of any strategic marketing plan. Rainmaking is phase two, but without knowing and managing your retention rate, rainmaking is for naught. The economic environment and the "total quality" movement have created heavy client/buyer leverage.

Familiarity

Client retention rate, not new client acquisition or market share, is the fundamental driver of profits.[1] That statement has a closet full of implications which, unrecognized, will rob a practice of growth possibilities. Consider a few facts:

- A 5 percent improvement in retention rate will improve profits 15-50 percent,[2]
- It is six times more expensive to get a new client than to retain a present client,[3]
- Clients leave because of perceived inattention, not fees,[4]
- A dissatisfied client will tell 8 to 10 people about his problem, and one in five will tell 20.[5]

The primary implication of retention as a driver of profits is structural: View a client base as having three tiers: profitable (level one), mildly profitable (level two, conjecture) and not so profitable (level three, by popular vote).

Level one clients may or may not demand the most attention, but they should be given the most time. They are the best source of cross-selling opportunities, and they will send excellent referrals who have better than average retention rates and cost nothing. Focus on developing cross-selling abilities and referral-based revenues.

This tiered structure demands regulation of the amount of attorney time devoted to level two and three clients by managing the process of client contact. For example, if a level three client calls with a question, an associate may be an appropriate respondent, not a partner. At the same time, level two's ought to be reviewed for growth or cross-selling possibilities. Moving even a small percentage up to the first level will have a significant impact.

Restructuring the way the client base is viewed and responded to implies that more people in the firm will have contact with clients. Therefore, continual quality training and review of both the procedures and the substance of client interactions is required. For example, establishing a routine review with attorneys and staff of types of situations that get delegated both up and downstream works to smooth time requirements and address liability issues.

Interview Clients

The second major structural implication of the notion that retention rates drive profits is that continual and comprehensive feedback mechanisms between firm and client must be established. Level one's will usually leave the firm silently, not because of price, but because of perceived indifference shown by someone at the firm.[6] Without studied and assertive communication, asking and listening by formal and informal means, the keeper of the keys exits stage left without notice. *Ergo exeunt profits.*

If top clients leave mostly due to controllable causes, what are the remedies? Rigorously managed, two-way client communications are critical. First, target a quarterly communication (newsletter, survey, client focus group, client function) and ask: "How do you evaluate our firm's service?" "How can we increase our service to you?" "Do you know that we do X? Do you (or anyone you know) have any interest in X?"

What the best clients tell you about their perception of your work is the sine qua non of marketing advice: to influence other prospective clients, use the advice of experts — your clients.

Beyond this first level of inquiry, regular reviews with the client are called for by the fundamentally intangible nature of professional services. The value of such intangible service is quickly forgotten. Clients remember the benefit, but the dollar and sense value is progressively hazier over time unless your worth is revalidated. This review and revalidation also establishes a platform for cross-selling and earning referrals.

Secondly, client complaints or negative incidents should be handled by the person in charge as fast as possible, and in a nonconfrontational manner. Whether the issue is fees, procedures or results, the highest level attorney should respond and negotiate a resolution within 24 hours.

At issue in these imbroglios is the core of profitability, and hence your growth: negative referral evidence conservatively predicts that an ex-client tells 8 to 10 other people. Lastly, client unrest triggers a perceived negative incident which will require 12 positive experiences to overcome.[7] Consider the reputation damage, much less the cost implications, and priorities crystallize.

As a practical matter, if you managed retention rates and therefore earned high-quality referrals and expanded fees from present clients, you might never have to rainmake again. Think about it: no bad chicken dinners, no more stranger-filled rooms, no more speeches at the Mordant Morticians Association of America.

Reality is, though, that retention rates are never 100 percent. As well, new clients expand the intellectual boundaries of a practice and cushion economic downturns. The pursuit of absolute growth requires earnest rainmaking efforts in addition to managing client retention rates.

Client retention tactics are the first phase of a strategic marketing program that yields growth. Then rainmaking follows naturally.

* * * *

1. Reichheld, Frederick F. and Sasser, W. Earl, "Zero Defections: Quality Comes to Service," *Harvard Business Review*, Sept.-Oct. 1990, p. 105.
2. *Ibid.,* p. 105-107.
3. Sellers, Patricia.
4. *U.S. News and World Report,* Nov. 11, 1991.
5. Goodman, John, Technical Assistance Research Programs Inc., "Measuring the Grapevine, Consumers Response and Word of Mouth," 1986.
6. *Op. cit., U.S. News and World Report.*
7. *Op. cit.*, Goodman.

Christine S. Filip *is an attorney and president of Success Consulting, a consulting firm for attorneys based in New York.*

Reprinted with the permission of the

The Suffolk Lawyer

A Publication of The Suffolk County Bar Association

Improving Cash Flow In Your Practice

By Christine S. Filip

Cash flow is customarily defined as net income plus depreciation. As practitioners, however, we know cash flow on more intimate terms — what I call "cash slow." This phenomenon is described to me almost daily as I consult with law firms.

You know the cash slows: net thirty becomes net sixty, clients astonished into parsimony when they find out the balance owed, others who hassle you, vendors attempting to accelerate collection by trying to tack on penalty charges, needed funds in your bank unavailable because an out-of-state check has not yet cleared.

Problems with cash flow are a leading factor in the failure of practices and businesses alike. If you don't have a financial wizard managing the economic status of your practice, cash flow management is in your hands, or on your shoulders. Here are some straightforward methods of managing your most important asset: cash.

1. **Talk about terms of payment and projected costs during your first consultation.** Clients have told me that they prefer to have this information early because it reduces anxiety, even if the numbers are large. My research also indicates that it paves the way for faster payment because the payment issue becomes integrated into the working relationship *ab initio*. You will need to present reminders: your engagement letter should be specific on the topic, your (monthly) invoices should have clear terms printed on them, you should be discussing overdue balances with clients quickly and in a nonconfrontational manner, e.g., "Is there any way I can be helpful in structuring your payment . . ."
2. **Collect faster by using positive incentives and alternative billing methods.** Few clients respond favorably to penalty charges for late payment, but some will take advantage of early payment opportunities if they make financial sense. To facilitate payment on extended, costly work, consider interim payments based on projected budgets; your client will have a realistic forecast that will help him or her mar-

shal funds. Time is money: a 40-day lag in collection of a $10,000 invoice means a loss of $45 in interest earnings at 4 percent. Small amount until you start multiplying.

3. **Disburse slowly using separate payables account.** Negotiate with your vendors/creditors to achieve best payment terms possible. All terms are negotiable, and best terms are the prize of those who ask. When you do disburse money, use a separate account, such as a zero balance account. Reason being, you do not want to keep balances above your payables amount in an account which makes no money.
4. **Improve the availability of your funds by negotiating with your bank.** Getting fixed availability on your checks eliminates the check float that can be as high as 7 days on out-of-state checks; ensure same-day availability on cash deposits and electronic payments such as wire transfers. Your bank will have an availability schedule which will enumerate terms. If your banker is less than enthusiastic about your request, either talk with the branch manager or speak with another bank. Availability schedules change so check with your bank at least every quarter.
5. **Concentrate your funds and get better information.** Your funds will be more productive in one bank by boosting interest earnings. You should get daily information on cash inflows and outflows from your bank — by phone, by fax or by computer. If you don't know the status of your cash, you cannot make informed financial decisions. Poor cash flow is one of the fastest ways to sink your practice.

Editor's Note: Attorney Christine S. Filip is the president of The Success Group, a Manhattan-based marketing company for law firms.

Reprinted with the permission of the

Massachusetts Lawyers Weekly

July 19, 1993 Lawyer-To-Lawyer Referral Guide

WHEN CLIENTS DISSENT

By Christine S. Filip

"I've decided to work with another firm," says your most profitable client. "But I thought we had settled our differences," you respond. "No, I disagree. Things are still the same and for too long now." Click.

Does this scenario wake you up at night? Have you mused lately that you are not sure what clients want anymore? Losing clients — especially profitable ones — will gut the profitability of your practice, causing high operating costs from turnover and marketing expenses.

The causes of client dissent are surprising and controllable. Clients don't leave because of fees or other seemingly concrete issues. Clients leave due to perceived indifference exhibited by someone at your firm.[1] Indifference leads to dissent and in turn to defection.

Indifference has as many faces as there are exceptions to the rule against hearsay. Indifference may be the slow response on your part to a client's question. What's slow? Ask a client about response time — often it differs from your notion of time.

Indifference may be not explaining the steps you have taken on your client's behalf. Your hours of labor may be transparent to the client. The phone call returned two days later, not today, may be seen as indifference. Indifference may be perceived rudeness on the part of your staff, such as questioning incoming callers as though they have to prove their worthiness to speak with you. With four or five of these "negative" incidents, you and your staff have proved your indifference. The client leaves, fails to give you a referral or speaks negatively about your firm. You'll need three new clients to replace this lost profit stream.

Managing Retention Rates Means Measurement

On a positive note, client dissent flows from highly remediable behaviors and miscues in your relationship. At the same time, the financial motivation to manage loyalty factors is clear. Boosting your client retention rate has serious implications for profitability: a 5 percent improvement in retention rates can boost profits 15 to 50 percent.[2] The most profitable firms have a retention rate of 93 to 95 percent whereas the average firm has a 78 to 85 percent retention rate.[3] Managing the process takes planning and behavioral change for both attorneys and staff. Measurement, setting goals and review is the starting point.

Indifference leads to dissent and in turn to defection.

If retention rates drive profitability, managing the process of loyalty has three key issues:

1. Pay keen attention to your most profitable clients. If you think about your client base in three levels (very profitable, sort of and not so profitable), spend the most time and expense with your most profitable — the level one's.

   This means that both you and your staff need clear-cut procedures to know when to delegate client questions and issues upstream and down. Client dissent (even if you think it's piffling) should trigger strict liability for nonconfrontational negotiation with the client. Should we be slaves to overreaching client demands? Clearly, no. Every dissent does not require concessions. Mere acknowledgment and explanation serves to dissolve many portentous bubbles of conflict, however.
2. Stay in touch and listen actively. Like any important relationship in your life, building loyalty requires that you integrate communication and feedback systems with clients, staff (your early warning system) and you. Phone calls, surveys, newsletters, client functions, thank you notes and focus groups all serve this purpose.
3. Find out why clients defect. They will tell you and usually in easy-to-grasp terms. Understanding the specifics of causation can directly shape better retention behaviors on your part. It's uncomfortable but anytime a client defects, or even complains, the attorney in charge of the matter should inquire immediately for specifics. Any possibility of a negotiated solution must occur quickly if it is to work. Any person in your office should be able to launch a "problem alert" form for your immediate attention. The form should have specific facts, statements and questions listed. It ought to be a bright color to provoke notice and it should be answered to the client's satisfaction within 24 hours. Being in court, on a trip or in conference are not roadblocks to resolution. If you can't get to the phone directly, have an associate immediately schedule a phone appointment between you and the client.

Retention and Rainmaking Are Linked

Managing retention and expanding your practice through rainmaking are two sides of the same coin: growth strategies. Retention is the requisite, though, because the cost of finding new clients is so high — five to six times the expense of servicing a present client.[4] A focus on new client acquisition alone will drive up operational costs.

The remedy to client dissent and defections stems from aggressive two-way communication with clients, enhanced feedback from staff and speedy treatment of seemingly insignificant client complaints.

Good clients are partners in profit margin production. Loyal clients are your best source of new fee revenues from cross-selling and they provide the highest quality, loyal referrals. A referral from a loyal client has a 92 percent retention rate versus 68 percent from advertising.[5] On the other hand, defecting clients will tell 8 to 10 people and one in five will tell 20.[6] The result is evident: the grapevine is stronger than any advertising or marketing campaign you launch.

Endnotes

1. *U.S. News and World Report*, Nov. 11, 1991.
2. Reichheld, Frederick F. and Sasser, W. Earl, "Zero Defections: Quality Comes to Service," *Harvard Business Review*, Sept.-Oct. 1990, pp. 105-107.
3. Reichheld, Frederick F. and Shea, Mary Beth, "Customer Retention Strategies," The Planning Forum's International Conference, Toronto, Canada, April 30, 1991.
4. Sellers, Patricia, "Getting Customers to Love You," *Fortune* magazine, March 13, 1989, p. 38.
5. *Op. cit.*, Reichheld and Shea.
6. Goodman, John, Technical Assistance Research Programs, Inc., "Measuring the Grapevine, Consumers Response and Word of Mouth," 1986.

Christine S. Filip, an attorney, is the president of Success Consulting, a Manhattan-based consulting firm for attorneys.

Reprinted with the permission of the

Brooklyn Barrister

Vol. 44 No. 3 March, 1993 A Publication of the Brooklyn Bar Association

WHAT DO CLIENTS WANT, ANYHOW?

Christine S. Filip, Esq.*

Ah, rainmaking! Powerfully persuasive lawyers attract clients like magnets without a drop of sweat being shed. The less fortunate of the profession are left the remains. If only the secret of such attraction were known.

It is. The answer is in asking open questions of clients, which is a task I often perform ancillary to my practice. The questions have to do with why clients choose to work with one attorney over another; what traits led them to believe they wanted to go forward with Attorney X instead of Attorney Y; why they remain loyal, and why they don't. The responses to these queries yield a treasure trove of information which should shape our behavior in two areas critical to the success of a practice: (1) how you acquire new clients, and (2) how you retain good clients because retention is the single most important factor in supporting profitable, growing practices.

And the Answer Is . . .

"Comfort level" first. When clients are asked to specify the reasons for selecting a lawyer, they almost always talk about feeling comfortable with the person behind the desk. They recount how they felt about the quality and tone of the interaction, as well as their treatment by other contact personnel. It is through the prism of interpersonal skills that they evaluate or speculate, even, how well you will perform on their behalf. It is rapport, that fragile bridge between people, that leads clients to you, and leads them away.

But what of competence? Reputation? Keen intellect and perspicacious judgment? These fall in priority behind the comfort level indicators mentioned above. Competence is often assumed: the referral by a colleague or family member satisfies the initial criterion. What is important is that the interpersonal criteria are paramount in both individual buyers of legal services and business buyers. On both sides of the marketplace, prospective clients respond that unless or until competence became an issue, they had to feel assured that the relationship with the attorney was one with which they felt comfortable.

Unpacking the Comfort Suitcase

What do these responses indicate to the acquisition of new clients? Specifically, how prospective clients get to know you is critical. If we start at the beginning of the marketing or rainmaking process, your participation in the community or professional networks of the prospective client is important. As professionals we are our own billboards. What appears on the billboard ought to be well thought out. The court of public opinion demands as reasoned a strategy as any complex litigation would require.

The setting where prospective clients meet you to discuss their legal business is the next forum we usually have to influence the choice process. Put yourself in the prospective client's shoes in your office. What do you see, and how would you want to be treated by each person you meet in that office? Now, dig in deeper: If you were the one going to part with what you thought was a bundle of money, would you consider the intake treatment and the relationship with the attorney good enough to pay the bill?

Should I Go, Or Should I Stay??

If you think about the lifetime value of a client, retention becomes a paramount issue. Firms with higher than average retention rates are more profitable: loyal clients give referrals, and the lack of client churn vividly reduces operating costs. They also win and retain clients despite the presence of lower cost competitors. When a client leaves, you will need to find three more to replace the revenue and profit stream, and it will cost you six times as much.[1] Thus, the cost of churning your client base is onerous.

Fortunately, it takes four to five negative incidents before a client will leave you. Most exit silently, with, I am sure, some notable exceptions. Unhappy clients tell eight to ten other people, and one in five will tell twenty.[2] There goes the billboard.

If getting new clients springs from interpersonal comfort levels, keeping clients does also. The wise attorney stays in touch with clients, and builds feedback loops into the ordinary course of client relationships. When differences occur ("I don't like how you handled X!") or indifference happens (the bill isn't paid), you have a better shot at retaining the client if you negotiate the differences rather than attacking or defending. Secondarily, your office personnel often sense when a client is miffed; they should be your early warning system.

But What of Competence . . . Keen Judgment . . . Perspicacity??

As attorneys, we ought not substitute our standards of professional competence for the selection criteria of clients. They select a person with an assumed or reported competence; we see legal acumen, or lack thereof, then the person. This is not to diminish the ever-growing sophistication of the buying public in any way. It is the order of the selection criteria, interpersonal attributes first, that illuminates the inside of the rainmaking machine.

* * * *

1. Sellers, Patricia, "Getting Customers to Love You," *Fortune* magazine, March 13, 1989, p. 38.

2. Goodman, John, Technical Assistance Research Programs, Inc., "Measuring the Grapevine, Consumers Response and Word of Mouth," 1986.

**Christine S. Filip is an attorney and the president of Manhattan-based Success Consulting.*

Reprinted with the permission of the

Bergen Barrister

December 1992 The publication of the Bergen County Bar Association

How to Boost the Profitability of Your Practice

by Christine S. Filip

Does the thought of doing marketing tasks make you feel tired, slightly nauseated, a victim of entropy, and frustrated? If you've been out trying to make rain by finding brand new clients, you probably feel those ways. In contrast, if you want to dramatically improve the profitability and growth of your practice this year, you need to focus your efforts first on your best **present** clients, creating an ongoing interchange that answers three levels of inquiry tacitly and explicitly:

1. **Evaluative Information:** How do you evaluate the quality of our service?
2. **Expansive Information:** How else may we be of service to you or to your colleagues, your association, your friends (by referral)?
3. **Open-ended Information:** What suggestions do you have concerning our service offerings? Our treatment of you? Our future working relationship?

When these questions are institutionalized into all your client communications and conversations, you will increase the loyalty of your clients, thereby significantly boosting profits. This dynamic interrelationship between loyalty and profits occurs because present clients are without acquisition costs, so their continuing work is incremental revenue, no expense. And broadly managed two-way communication ensures that the bridge of loyalty and rapport is maintained, and information is current for both parties.

Loyalty Drives Profitability

The rationale for initiating your rainmaking efforts on your best clients first has to do with economics and professionalism. When your best clients stay loyal — they come back with the next matter, or for new services, or they refer someone to you — they critically influence profitable growth to the extent that a 5% increase in client loyalty boosts profits 15 to 50%.[1] Referrals have a 92% loyalty versus 68% from advertising. Furthermore, when you remove the causes of client dissatisfaction, you eliminate pervasive negative word of mouth advertising that will be hard to overcome. Finally, it is your best ("Level One") clients who provide close to 80% of your fee revenues; when one leaves you'll have to replace that client with three new ones to replace lost dollars, and you'll spend a lot of time doing so.

In real terms, were you to ignore this economic reality, you could go to a networking function every night of the week, face roomfuls of unknown folks who seem to be part of a secret club, eat chicken, maybe some peas, and still not have any new clients for a long time. Crankiness sets in.

In contrast, were you to go eat chicken with an association one of your best clients attends, say the Mordant Morticians Association, you would meet a room full of prospects whose legal needs are familiar. Positioning your competence center stage in such a milieu is a fertile marketing theatre.

Count Your Blessings

The management of any economic proposition requires analysis in your practice. The first step is to segment your clients into groups that are manageable. Most client bases fall (grossly) into three categories: profitable clients whose work you enjoy (Level One), marginal clients who seem to have some expansion probabilities and pay their bills (Level Two), and those you'd rather forget, but you can't because they always call despite slow paying patterns (Level Three).

The first order of action is to scrutinize the fall-out, or defection, during the last 12 months of your Level One clients and derive your retention rate. Manage this number, and notice changes when you implement loyalty management techniques. Next, wherever possible, find out why good clients left; they will have very concrete reasons. Use those reasons to strike negative behaviors, and to guide your future marketing tactics.

On an ongoing basis, when clients dissent, are disgruntled, or hold misconceptions, fix these problems fast; don't delegate them or drag your feet responding. With problems solved quickly, these clients remain loyal. Swept under the rug, these "insignificant" complaints come home to roost as ethical complaints in the worst case, and always become negative advertising.

Encouraging Loyalty/Counteracting Defection

As in any human alliance, high-quality, two-way communication increases the value of the relationship. What it takes to support loyalty is to change expectable communication patterns in your practice so that good information flows to all parties.

From my experience interviewing Level One legal clients, the communication pattern I am about to suggest fits with what clients want from their professional relationships. Grossly generalized, clients want better relationship values ("understanding my goals" or "my business," "treats me as an equal") and higher quality communication ("I hear from them," "returns my calls," "thoroughly discusses alternatives"). When asked, they are attracted by the quality of the relationship, intelligent service, and less influenced by price. As one client put it, "Do you shop the price of neurosurgery?"

Here are some examples of structuring your client communications around evaluative, expansive, and open-ended inquiries so that loyalty and profitability come to the fore:

- **Evaluative Data:** Short written surveys can be sent with invoices, asked informally, sent as a fax-back-in newsletter, or under separate cover periodically. **Tacit Issue:** How do you evaluate the quality of our service?
- **Expansive Data:** As part of a survey, newsletter, focus group, account review, or any client interaction, expanding the ways you can be of greater service is up to you to initiate. **Preplan your calls** to fertile clients incorporating suggestions for future matters, a preventive analysis, and signal your willingness to talk to (**referred**) colleagues. If your client is active in a **professional association**, ask to attend, become a member if appropriate, and take an active role speaking or writing for the group. **Tacit Issue:** How else may we be of service to you or to your colleagues?
- **Open-ended Data:** Whenever, and however, you ask for feedback from clients, make sure that you leave time for the "suggestion box," i.e., the open-ended question. You will get high-quality information. **Tacit Issue:** What are your suggestions concerning our services, treatment of you, and our future working relationship?

These interactions should be carefully planned so that you get a consistent stream of good information and position yourself, as a result, for cross-selling opportunities and referrals.

Loyalty, Redux

Pay close attention to your Level One clients. Know them as best you can, seek ways to further the interchange, and listen closely. Keeping them will drive down the operational costs of your practice, and the frustration of continually seeking new clients.

Footnote

1. Reichheld, Frederick F. and Sasser, W. Earl, "Zero Defections: Quality Comes to Service," *Harvard Business Review,* Sept.-Oct. 1990, p. 105.

Reprinted with the permission of the

New Jersey Lawyer

Volume 1, Number 48 December 21, 1992

Law Firm Marketing

DISCOVERING WHY CLIENTS CHOOSE YOU

By Christine S. Filip

"Everyone makes a living by selling something," Robert Louis Stevenson wrote more than 100 years ago.

But most of us don't think about our clients buying our services. And we probably admit less to the notion of selling.

Why clients "buy" — that is, why and how they choose to work with one lawyer over another — is an illustration of buying criteria, that scoreboard in the arena of persuasion that happens in the head of the prospective client.

"What clients tell you about why they choose you is the most fertile marketing advice you might hear. It is the most valid indicator of selection data and your perceived value."

— Christine S. Filip

In breaking the scoring down to its component bits, one can find patterns, trends, and useful ways in which to mold future actions.

Should we care about buying criteria? You bet. It is the only advice that counts.

When you know the reasons why clients have chosen to work with you, you can find other clients with similar criteria or needs. When you analyze the reasons why clients have chosen you, you will know how to address these criteria during the selection process of prospective clients. Thus you influence the prospect to choose you.

If the client's needs cannot be met, or your capabilities don't fit with the client or the matter, you will both see this early on.

What clients tell you about why they choose you is the most fertile marketing advice you might hear. It is the most valid indicator of selection data and your perceived value.

The problem is that most times, these questions are not asked. Without this critical advice, one may proceed on supposition to build a client development program, which, yielding marginal results, will show that marketing has limited value to the profession.

Non-Adversarial Discovery

If you ask your clients the right questions, they will tell you about the first level criteria — what I call comfort level indicators.

A client will say they heard about you from a friend and felt comfortable when they met with you. Dig a little deeper and you will hear evidence of reputation and competence. The word-of-mouth reference carries weight, and both you and your office environment appeared competent. How the space looks, how people interact within it and how you appear are crucial comfort level indicators.

You don't need a marketing maven to uncover this information. You don't need a formalized, statistically valid sample and a questionnaire to begin the process. You need only to have good communication with your clients — the kind of discussion that probes not only legal issues at hand, but the process of selecting an attorney.

"How did you get my name?" "What specifically are you looking for in an attorney?" "What is most important to you in choosing an attorney?" "The last time you used a lawyer, what did you most appreciate about the services?" These are examples of discovery questions which shine light on buying criteria. This isn't hard to do and can be very helpful to a lawyer.

But during the course of your interaction with a client, things can get murky. As opposed to buyers of goods, buyers of services have an opportunity to say "no" almost anytime.

"No" sounds like: "Where is the letter you said you would send?" "Haven't you done anything on my case yet?" "I called you two days ago. Why haven't you returned my call? Did my secretary lose the phone message?"

Because of this dynamic, you have to keep checking the criteria as your relationship lengthens. This flies in the face of human nature. We tend to pay less and less attention to the choices the buyer has the longer we know them.

Revisit and Revalidate

Because things change, it is best to revisit the criteria on a timely basis. This is not necessarily a formalistic process. Chat over a meal. Use reviewing the relationship with your important clients as an opportunity to rediscover, and as an opportunity to look prospectively at your working relationship.

How will you be of service in the future? What has changed in the client's life since you initiated your relationship?

With a current perspective, you can expand the menu of services that you can offer. Cross-selling opportunities are embedded in this process. The divorce client may now need estate planning. The litigation client might now be buying a house.

Times change, and so do criteria. The client whose primary concern was survival two years ago will probably have new concerns today. If you don't know them well, you can't serve them. And, if you don't know them, someone else will.

Since the economics of replacing present clients are onerous — you need three new ones to replace the one you lose — skipping the revalidation process of client management is dangerous.

Criteria into Tactics

Using the information you gain about buying criteria, whether from the initial selection or later on, is the engine of the marketing process. Translating buying criteria into tactics — what you do to meet client needs — facilitates success and eliminates wasted efforts.

Simply put, if your clients want red autos, don't sell green ones. If your corporate clients generally say they are looking for high-quality work with a cost-containment flair, consistently demonstrate evidence of these criteria while listening for changes. Remember, the mix or rank order of the criteria may shift.

Let me illustrate some examples of wasted efforts. Over the last five years, newsletters have come into vogue in the professional service sector — particularly with lawyers and certified public accountants. Their effectiveness as a means of staying close to clients has decreased. There are too many newsletters, and many never get read.

Many times, clients don't even know you sent out a newsletter. Just look at your own desk. You probably receive more newsletters than you will ever have time to read.

Conclusion

Get to know your clients and frame your responses based on the criteria that interest them. Target your tactics, craft your language and you will enhance your success.

Christine S. Filip is president of New York-based Success Consulting, a management consulting firm for attorneys.

Reprinted with the permission of the

New Jersey Lawyer

Volume 1, Number 17 May 18, 1992

Law Firm Marketing

LAWYERS AREN'T JUST FOR EMERGENCIES ANYMORE

By Christine S. Filip

A good friend of mine who is a noted and successful certified public accountant is fond of making the analogy that accountants are the obstetricians of the professional world, while lawyers are the pathologists with all the attendant negative connotations.

He'll smile convincingly as he recounts how his best clients call him weekly to discuss business and personal matters, and wouldn't think of making a major financial decision without seeking out his advice. He adds that these same clients grit their teeth and wait until the last possible moment before calling their lawyer. He says they hate being "on the clock" with counsel.

Is this man all wet, or do we attorneys willingly cast ourselves as dragon slayers to be set aside when the fire-breathing monster is caged?

My experience as a consultant to lawyers and accountants teaches me that there is much to be learned and earned from the consultative role that my friend has fulfilled for his clients. His practice is strong and profitable. He's constantly referred to new clients by his present ones. And he seems to have a few good laughs on the way to the bank.

Give Year-Round Service

There is no singular secret of success which propels my friend. Rather, there is a consistent pattern of consultative behavior which is easy to learn, but hard to practice each and every day.

What all successful "rainmakers" have in common is the ability to make paying for advice palatable and worthwhile, even, in the eyes of their clients. It starts by knowing your client, by asking questions, and then marketing benefits to fit the needs you've uncovered. Let's take a closer look at the process.

When was the last time you enjoyed paying your taxes? "Never!" is the correct answer. None of us do because by April 15th we feel like we are paying for nothing, and "nothing" is the operative word.

With clients, the same process occurs upon receiving a bill for a phone or other conversation with you during which you know you imparted worthy advice. Perhaps there was preparation time as well. What does the client feel he or she should pay? Correct; nothing. Why?

Typically, they do not know what went into your time, and mostly they don't remember the conversation as a momentous event, or even a slightly important event for which a payment is due.

While I am stretching the point here, I want to illuminate the marketing process that drives a client's willingness to pay: value. When clients value the service, they pay willingly. The value button lights up when the client sees that you have met his needs with real service.

How does the notion of value help extend the billable hour? First, if you want to make it easy for a client to pay for advice, you have to impart tangibility — make it a real product.

Something Clients Can Touch

Real products get tangibility when you articulate a list of benefits, and a good reason to buy them that strikes home and makes good business sense. This takes lots of questions and selling time with your client. When you ask questions, you understand your clients' world and priorities. If you don't know a client's priorities, you have limited ways to address legal needs. What you can offer is a narrow slice of services. Questions, particularly open questions, expand the purview.

Last, but never least, any product you or I would buy has a price. While it is hard to put a price on legal matters, a ballpark estimate is better than nothing, and a thorough understanding of your billing (pricing) process allows the client to be a knowledgeable buyer.

On another level, legal advice becomes a product — something a client will more willingly pay for — when it's denoted as such in a letter or brochure. In the brochure, "advice" is more real if it's in a picture or illustration since words are more conceptual. If you've had the phone conversation, follow it up with a short written recap. It now has tangible form.

As a professional, you know the value of advice, especially when it is prospective and preventative. Looking forward into the future with a client rather than reacting to past events is fertile ground for expanding your services to clients.

To start this process of consultative marketing, you have to plan time with your clients. Calling current clients to discuss future needs and time availability will trigger this strategic process. This allows you to do two things: ascertain the scope of the client's needs, and prepare to service them.

This phone call or letter can also have a negative impact. For example, you might discover that your favorite client is no longer your client, or that the client is moving to a new jurisdiction. But, better to discover such things than not to know them.

During the course of this phone call or the ensuing conversation, take time to expand the menu of services that the client can choose from. For instance, with changes in the law, or new regulations taking effect, the business client may need you to run a seminar or workshop for key employees, revise contracts, or institute new procedures.

Listen to Clients

Since many law firms are giving seminars these days, take time to do something different: develop the seminar or other consultative interaction with the client, not just for the client. You will have a far better product, as well as gain tremendous insight into the client's world.

Let me demonstrate. If you recently handled a collection matter for a manufacturer and noticed that the written contract of sale did not have clear terms of payment, you could advise the client that you need to redraw the contracts.

However, with some consultative insight from the vice president of sales, you might discover that the source of the problem is twofold: (1) the contracts do need revising and the sales team needs some training on articulating terms, but, (2) you may also discover that the commission program pays out before the receivables are collected, and you may also need to spend time on restructuring this important piece of company policy.

For the singular client, there may be changes in the client's life or family that should trigger your planning process.

Whomever the client is, before you call, plan what you are going to say, ask many questions, listen, and have some good reasons that the client should partake in your recommended course of action. The reasons should be in the client's frame of reference, speaking to the client's needs and priorities.

The magic of my accountant friend is not complicated. He practices it day by day. He questions, listens, and advises. His priorities match those of his clients.

This process of consultation continually expands valued opportunities to be of service to your clients. It matches client needs with your professional advice. And the match makes money.

Lawyer Christine S. Filip is president of New York-based Success Consulting, a management consulting firm for attorneys.

Reprinted with the permission of the

New Jersey Lawyer

Volume 1, Number 3 February 10, 1992

Law Firm Marketing

BEYOND RAINMAKING IN PROMOTING LAWYERS' SERVICES

By Christine S. Filip

Let's kill all the rainmakers!

That has a nicer ring to it. Isn't it better than that Shakespearean epithet? But it really is high time to toss the term rainmaking out of the lexicon of the legal business.

It holds us back for a variety of reasons. Common lore is that rainmaking is something that other people do. This fable sometimes includes the codicil that those other people who do it — unless they are very experienced in marketing — do so because they own a less than scintillating legal mind. Fable perhaps, but part truth, too.

All of the above doesn't square with three economic realities:

- Marketing is everybody's task in the firm;
- Law is a mature industry; and
- Marketing services is tricky business.

The concept of rainmaking as a primary means of getting clients is not only outdated, but too narrow to admit professional success. It continues the illusion that as lawyers we don't have to grapple on a working level with that messy business of being a business, as well as a profession. Wealth creation through business growth requires knowledge and use of the marketing process.

The Consequences of Maturity

The times require adaptation to changed circumstances. The economics lesson of 1991 is that mature markets impose new requirements. And the marketplace is more likely to continue evolving rather than revert to conditions of the past. Simply put, when consumers (potential clients) have too many choices (potential lawyers), they shop around and drive down the price. Clients demand more because with overexposure to the legal process, they have been educated, informed, and supplied with multiple look-alike choices for representation as well as increasingly tantalizing substitutes like alternative dispute resolution and legal insurance plans.

The genesis of this heavy buyer leverage means that attracting new clients must be instigated, not awaited. All members of a law firm are instrumental in marketing because all members, from receptionist to senior partner, are emblematic of the quality of your work whether you like it or not.

"All right," you say, "I know that!" But the question is: What's a busy attorney to do about it?

What to Do Next

To professionalize the process of marketing rather than denigrate the profession of lawyering requires knowledge and appropriate actions. Marketing has to be learned and used in the same manner that lawyers learned the rules of evidence. Without regular practice, the skill deteriorates. In addition, all members of a firm must be trained about their part in the marketing process.

A good starting point to acquiring power is to understand the landscape of mature markets and the problems of marketing intangible, knowledge-based services. Continuing legal education programs on marketing are informative, practical and concise.

For example, the New Jersey Institute for Continuing Legal Education will sponsor a series in March and April called "Rainmaking in a Drought." An increasing number of colleges, through continuing education departments, serve up evening courses of 10 sessions or less on marketing professional services.

These are grown-up courses taught by practitioners. In this setting, working professionals get hands-on knowledge without tests, grades and other educational paraphernalia.

Like any business process, the marketing process must be sustained. Putting someone in charge of it helps. Then inspect what you get. Marketing expenses and revenues must be reviewed on a regular basis just as you would with other financial reports. If the result of your marketing decisions is not a positive change on the top and bottom line, reevaluate and make changes. But remember, you won't see results overnight.

Buyer leverage is here to stay. The problem of marketing something you can't see remains. King Nebulous, the intangible partner of marketing legal services, has a few marketing rules:

1. Make it real.
2. Do it again.

Making the unique attributes of your firm real in marketing terms means using tangible objects to represent your practice. A brochure is

> **"The concept of rainmaking as a primary means of getting clients is not only outdated, but too narrow to admit professional success."**
>
> — Christine S. Filip

tangible. But look at most legal brochures and you see oceans of verbiage. Legal services are intangible to begin with. You can't kick a contract like you would the tires of a car. And you can't take an oral argument for a test drive.

Words are conceptual representations which continue the prolix obfuscation of your unique talents as a lawyer — as that sentence did. As a result, using pictures, icons, and illustrations in a brochure and lessening the verbiage is helpful. Arrange the text so that it invites readership. Lists and bold dots help.

Consider your audience. What is unique about your legal talent has to reach both the hearts and minds of the audience. Now consider your audience as a jury. You open and you present a closing argument in court. Putting aside the legal parameters, you give the jury multiple exposures to the evidence. Prospective clients need continual exposure to the evidence of your competence to remind them how valuable your services are. Current clients need reminders of your talent, too.

Evidence used to remind clients should be tangible. A letter that follows up a first consultation is real. With existing clients, a status report is real. People forget. In marketing parlance, an account review is reminder evidence. Whatever you call it, it is a good opportunity to review the past and consider the future as a valued advisor. Uncovering how you may be of service in the future expands the revenue generation of the client because it expands the options for interaction.

This process of following up attests to your professionalism at the same time. You are not merely the lawyer to bring in for trouble, you are the day-to-day legal consultant as well. Advisors are less dispensable. They touch and concern more areas of the client.

The Expanded Menu

The preceding paragraph portrays the lawyer as a consultant. This increased visibility is the subtle, but more precious gain from marketing.

Marketing is an interactive, contact sport. When you use it, you increase your dialogue with current as well as potential clients.

Lawyer Christine S. Filip is president of New York-based Success Consulting, a management consulting firm for attorneys.

Reprinted with permission from the

New Jersey Law Journal

Vol. CXXXVI-No. 2 Monday, January 10, 1994 136 N.J.L.J. 101

Rules Say Promotions Should Be Informational

By Christine S. Filip

On one of your trips to the office this week, you may have heard a law firm ad on the radio. Undoubtedly you see the ever-increasing display ads in newspapers and magazines of all sorts. If you have asked yourself whether these advertising efforts pay off, maybe you first need to take a trip to the movies.

On a hot and humid Saturday afternoon last summer, as a concession to my out-of-town guests, I found myself in a cool movie theater watching *Jurassic Park*.

By now, you've heard about the scene. And regardless of your feelings about the scene's comic-book-inspired gore, it is instructive on the topic of lawyers and advertising.

Here we go: In a new theme park, a deadly Tyrannosaurus Rex hops an electric fence, menacing scientists, two children, and a corporate lawyer, all of whom sit in useless four-wheel drive vehicles.

The cowardly corporate attorney abandons his colleagues (and the two small children) seeking refuge from the attack of the mighty dinosaur. The lawyer seeks shelter in a portable bathroom. Not a wise choice, but humorous for the moviegoers.

As the dinosaur sniffs out the cowering lawyer, the audience howled in delight. Children to my left and right chanted. When the monster wrecks the outhouse and devours the attorney, who feebly quivers on the throne before he becomes a meal, the audience started to applaud and hoot their approval.

This scene has raised cries of displeasure from lawyers across the country. Without debating the intent of this scene, it's fair to make at least one generalization about why the scene resonates for the audience: They're not keen on the legal profession.

In a television commercial, Miller Lite has a lawyer "roundup" ad, and the recent *National Law Journal* survey tells us that we are less respected than just about any group except for politicians, many of whom are lawyers anyway.

Bates, et al. v. State Bar of Ariz., 433 U.S. 350 (1977), was decided by the U.S. Supreme Court almost 15 years ago, effectively allowing attorneys to advertise. Is there a connection between the use of mass media to market legal services and the status of the profession?

What regulations must attorneys be aware of when advertising their services?

Public Vilification

Certainly the public's vilification of the profession highlights a broader issue in the context of promotional strategy (advertising being only one of many promotional choices): backlash.

Given the nature of the audience at large, the unconsidered use of advertising may have a negative effect, rather than fulfilling its proposed purpose of attracting and informing clients and spurring referrals. In this light, the *Jurassic Park* predator may be an unwitting stepchild of the legal profession.

With ever-increasing numbers of people using the services of lawyers, does advertising per se serve the consumer? "Yes," says Israel David Dubin, secretary of the state Supreme Court's Committee on Attorney Advertising, "to the extent that it makes consumers aware of certain legal rights they might otherwise be unaware of . . . including areas of practice and fees for services."

Dubin points out, however, that New Jersey attorneys must be aware of the quite-specific Rules of Professional Conduct (RPC 7.1 through 7.5 are instructive) and of the committee's opinions and guidelines. Since New Jersey's rules vary from its neighbors', and interjurisdictional relationships invariably arise, "Many attorneys admitted to more than one bar must exercise great care to insure that advertising that reaches New Jersey residents complies with our rules," Dubin adds.

Should you be advertising? Yes, if your clients do not select professionals like you by querying their trusted colleagues for a referral, and if your clients usually come to you for one matter only.

You can reach mass audiences of first-time buyers by advertising, and intelligently written and placed ads minimize the costs of acquiring new clients. You also can remind former clients to refer others to you if you remain in their consciousness, through public exposure, for extended periods.

What you should know is that clients attracted through advertising have a loyalty rate of 68 percent against a 92 percent rate for clients referred by another client. Frederick F. Reichheld and W. Earl Sasser, "Zero Defections: Quality Comes to Service," *Harvard Business Review*, p. 107, (September-October 1990).

This is not a negative if the client comes to you just once in his or her lifetime and your operational structure matches this economic model, that is, your office can accommodate a higher volume of clients churned through with a strict eye to monitoring and reducing the costs of operations.

Promotional strategy is a business proposition, and it is imperative that you understand the economic engine that moves it along best and the importance of careful preparation. Fundamentally, the management of client loyalty, not market share, new client volume, not price, drives profitability. A 5 percent increase in client retention — measured in repeat business or referrals — will increase profits 15 percent to 50 percent. Ibid., at 105.

When your promotional strategy correlates with the economics of loyalty management, and reinforces how your most loyal clients chose you, you get the best economic payback. Here's an illustration: if your best clients came to you by reading a billboard (as permitted by CAA Opinion 3, 120 N.J.L.J. 1112 (Dec. 10, 1987), buy more billboard and other public display advertising, e.g., space in community newspapers.

Conversely, let's say that you serve business clients doing (expensive) commercial litigation and you place a display ad in the newspaper, which nets you two calls from start-ups with relatively little cash. In hindsight, you can see that your best clients were word-of-mouth referrals from current clients.

The lesson is that you are helping yourself most if you spend your promotional dollars on activities that develop referral sources: social functions, face-to-face briefings, or client functions that advance legitimate business interests while displaying your professional competence and personality.

The client not suited to your practice, or treated indifferently by anyone at your firm, will defect. A dissatisfied client will express that dissatisfaction to 8 to 10 other people, and one in five will tell 20. John Goodman, Technical Assistance Research Programs, Inc., "Measuring the Grapevine, Consumers' Response and Word of Mouth," 1986.

Do you suppose there were any of those broadcasters in the *Jurassic Park* movie audience?

Understand Advertising's Impact

Given these statistics, a good place to begin is in understanding where advertising will have the most positive financial impact: with your current clients for cross-selling and referral power, and with their analogues, i.e., similarly situated prospects.

For example, if your clients come from a geographic area, you can advertise for further penetration in that geographic market and also in other "geographies" where similar prospects live (analogues).

Advertising is defined as a paid promotional message, such as a display ad in a periodical or a broadcast advertisement. It is, however, only one subset of your promotional choices, which include face-to-face selling; personal marketing through community involvement or professional and trade association membership; distribution of newsletters, surveys and brochures; and client functions like briefings, seminars and social events.

The most persuasive messages about your firm's worthiness come from the mouths of those you've served. But ads using testimonials may best be left to informal 'word of mouth.'

Advertising's purpose is to engender a positive response in its target audience, to help the reader/listener make a choice based on a persuasive message. Your best return comes from aiming your promotional dollars at current clients to promote repurchases ("We handled your first sensitive negotiation, and we want to remind you to call us the next time" via a law-firm newsletter or luncheon); exploiting cross-selling opportunities ("We handled your divorce and now we'd like to handle your estate planning" via newsletter, brochure, or social function); and mining similar prospects ("We're experienced in your business/profession" via a display ad in a trade journal).

Note that CAA Opinion 7, 127 N.J.L.J. 753 (March 21, 1991), limits words describing expertise to the more informational descriptions, like "concentrated in." Otherwise, a specialist certification is required.

Spending money on the familiar and their analogues (repurchasers) makes good economic sense. Doing what you know best is more profitable than continually scouting out new types of clients.

The second order of advertising focus is to aim your current services at new market segments (cross-selling). For example, if you have done other product-liability cases and you might now advertise to attract breast-implant cases.

Last on the economic payback scale is promoting new services to new markets. For example, you've brought in a new practice group and are going after clients different from those you've served in the past. This is the most expensive and risk-laden promotional activity.

This does not mean that you should not spend promotional dollars on getting new clients. It means that your economic payback may be smaller relative to other promotional contexts that spur referrals and cross-selling opportunities.

Intangibility of Legal Services

Promotional strategy is a communication function. Communicating about something as intangible as legal services is an especially difficult task. Unlike selling cars, legal services can't be test driven to help in the selection process. Nor can one kick the tires of a law firm.

Because of this, professional services ads are most effective when they encompass fewer words and more graphics that lend tangibility and promote understanding. For example, Prudential Insurance Co. of America's use of the Rock of Gibraltar imparts the notion of long-lasting solidity and sturdiness. Words, being conceptual, like services, tend to obfuscate in this context.

But, let the wise practitioner not forget the strictures of RPC 7.2, which stresses that advertising should be "predominantly informational" and without "animations, dramatizations, music or lyrics . . . used in connection with televised advertising."

The work of the legal profession turns on the use and interpretation of words spoken or written, while most of our nonlegal brothers and sisters are visually oriented. They think and see the world in visual images. As recipients of your promotional copy (ads, brochures, etc.), the typical reader will scan and selectively tune out large chunks of verbiage. Promotional copy, then, that uses graphics, bold print to set off major topics, and bullets invite the reader's interest.

The same is true of the profession's credentialing. It is best left to listing in the legal directory. Even sophisticated clients rarely care what law school you went to, and most have no idea what law review and clerking for a judge mean in terms of service quality. In promotional copy, those credentials are clutter.

The most persuasive messages about your worthiness come from the mouths of those you've served, by reference and testimonials. These are the most powerful marketing tools one can use, but given the nature of New Jersey's regulations, their use must be carefully crafted, and perhaps left to the informal "word of mouth" advertising that is indeed helpful.

Practitioners should note CAA Opinion 8, 127 N.J.L.J. 753 (March 21, 1991), which says you cannot repeat through the words of another in a testimonial that which you cannot say as an attorney, because it violates RPC 7.1(a)(3).

But, in a more recent opinion, CAA Opinion 15, 133 N.J.L.J. 1370 (April 5, 1993), holds that testimonials can be used with a disclaimer ("Results may vary depending on your particular facts and legal circumstances") in print and recited by a narrator on radio or television. In addition, the quoted material must be from an identifiable person who actually received those services.

Promotional Strategy

A solid and successful promotional strategy can and should encompass a wider range of choices than print and broadcast media, but if advertising is what you want to try, here are some guidelines.

Know as much about your target market as possible. The medium, message, timing, and frequency appropriate to your purposes turn on the audience you want to communicate with. Knowledge of the attributes of your intended audience is critical. Marketers call this demographic and psychographic information; age, educational levels, income, attitudes, occupation, as well as values and lifestyle details should advise your choice of medium.

For example, let's suppose that you wish to communicate with senior citizens about elder law issues. Demographic data might show you that seniors read and listen to the radio more than the general population. Therefore, choosing to place ads in local newspapers might be as effective as spending greater amounts of money on other media, such as television.

If your intended audience resides chiefly in certain counties, publish in those counties' papers, or use broadcast media whose greatest communication "reach" is in the geographic market that matches your target market.

Test your media choice from a variety of viewpoints. On the other hand, your knowledge of the habits and values of a sophisticated business/professional buyer of legal services might lead you to choose placement in more professional journals, drive-time business radio, late-night or early-morning television news.

Once you have selected some possible media placements, call up the advertising manager and ask to be sent a press kit, rate card for costs, and some recent samples if you are dealing with print media.

The press kit will have information about the readership, viewership or listenership, including facts about the outlet's audience, population statistics, publication dates, distribution or media-reach breakdowns and special issues. The rate card will specify advertising costs on a contract or noncontract basis, and additional services that the media can supply such as graphic art design, layout, typesetting, etc.

As a final check on whether you have selected an appropriate print or broadcast media, talk to some of their current advertisers and find out what results they have achieved. A similar type of firm, e.g., a professional service firm, might be able to tell you how many new clients or new matters they have garnered by advertising in the paper, broadcast media or magazine you are evaluating.

If this evaluation leads you to believe that the advertising vehicle is worthwhile, then buy the space or time for your ads. As a trial, you will want to advertise more than once; five or six publications will give you an adequate test run. You will want to have your staff track the source of new matters coming in to quantify the results of your ad campaign. If the results were worthwhile, consider continued placements.

Advertising, whether in print or broadcast media, falls into three broad categories. Institutional ads promote the attributes of the firm per se. This may be your firm's brochure, although it can certainly be the basis of an advertisement. The message may focus on depth of experience, or particular client services.

Most important, this type of institutional message must delineate the unique advantages of dealing with your firm. An overly general or broad message will have little effect. The use of institutional ads probably has the least effect for most firms in terms of payback, except if you are advertising to colleagues, or announcing new practice areas or a change of address.

Highlighting the Differences

Competitive ads point out how you or your firm is different from the rest of the pack. This highlighting of competitive advantage can be effective if planned carefully and ethically.

RPC 7.1(a)(3) prohibits comparisons between one lawyer's services and another's, and CAA Opinion 7, 127 N.J.L.J. 753 (March 21, 1991), limits articulation of areas of expertise to the "predominantly informational" format such as "My practice is concentrated in the field of," or to a statement regarding the certification as a specialist in a practice area.

Your advertising copy can communicate your firm's competitive advantages in other more persuasive ways. Competitive advantage, or the values your clients are willing to pay for, exists only in the mind of your clients. Therefore, your competitive ad must speak to the attributes your best clients value.

Before you write your ad, gather information from your best clients and focus on the most-valued attributes, and your copy will make a difference. Finally, reminder ads ("Don't leave home without it"), when they are effective, serve to reinforce repurchasers of your services.

Promotional strategy today is as much about the perception of the profession as it is about the portrayal of one firm's advantages. Given this context, and the economic lessons of loyalty management, the selection of messages and media is ethically and professionally critical.

The ethical context is rapidly shifting. In two opinions, CAA Opinion 13, 132 N.J.L.J. 267 (Oct. 5, 1992), and the Supplement to Opinion 13, 133 N.J.L.J. 652 (March 1, 1993), the use of cooperative and commercial advertising programs, which pool law firms' advertising efforts, must be accompanied by the disclaimer "Attorney Advertisement. (Name of Program) is not a law firm or lawyer referral service."

In the near term, the CAA is working on an opinion considering the advertising for and the use of 1-900 telephone numbers. And, as Dubin points out, "The so-called high-tech highway may also raise issues and give rise to problems never before considered."

The author is an attorney and the president of The Success Group in New York City, a marketing firm for professionals. She regularly presents marketing seminars for attorneys for the New Jersey Institute for Continuing Legal Education.

Reprinted with the permission of

Small Business Reports

September 1994 A Publication of the American Management Association

SELLING EXPERT AIR

By Christine S. Filip

All types of service providers face a tricky sales obstacle: How can they make their expert advice "real" for prospective clients?

Have you ever tried to "test drive" a financial advisor or kick the tires (much as you'd like to) of an attorney or computer consultant? Well, none of us can. All of these professionals sell advice of one sort or another — and that advice cannot be seen, tested or simonized by a prospective buyer.

That's a problem if your company is on the other side of the fence, selling professional services to prospects who cannot see or touch the "merchandise." No matter what type of service you offer, such as legal advice, accounting work, business consulting or travel planning, you must overcome a distinct sales disability — the product you sell is air. It may be very expert air, but it's air all the same.

The challenge is to give your expert air a more tangible form in the selling process. Certain sales tactics can help you accomplish that goal by making your service more "real" and allowing prospects to kick some tires before they make the purchasing decision. These tactics can enhance your closing ratio and make the sale less price sensitive. They'll also help you retain customers for a lifetime of repeat business and referrals — the ultimate drivers of profitability.

Giving Shape to Air

Let's start with a basic reality: While you have faith in the veracity of your sales pitch, prospective clients do not. They haven't had a chance to test-drive your services, so the adage that talk is cheap — and its corollary, people lie — control the sales presentation. You have to overcome those assumptions, and these tactics can help you do it:

Paint a colorful picture. If you ask most clients what they think of the services they've purchased, they will remember some tangible aspect of the experience — the invoice, the computer that didn't communicate across town or a letter outlining your work on their behalf. These are the "memory handles" clients use to recount the relationship. Your job is to create these handles for prospects as well, using two techniques: highly visual, graphic sales tools that support your pitch and real client stories that illustrate the benefits of your services. Both of these create a picture of your "expert air" and bring it into focus for the prospect.

The graphic sales tools can include brochures and other materials that have pictures, bold headlines and "bulleted" chunks of information, as well as computer programs and videotapes. Since we recall information in snapshots, not in words or data, these graphics allow you to slide information into prospects' memory banks. They can grasp the benefits of your service and recall them better, which means you'll spend far less time selling.

The adage that "talk is cheap" controls the initial sales presentation.

Consider the need for these visual aids from the prospect's point of view: While your sales pitch may reflect an adroit familiarity with all facets of your business, the prospect sits on the other side of the table thinking, "I don't know if I believe this guy...I wonder if he'll do what he says...Could I lose my job over this decision?" The prospect is right to be so skeptical. Using words alone, which are concepts in and of themselves, to explain another concept, your service, compounds the cloudiness of the picture. You need clarity and memorability.

A note of caution: The graphics and text must illustrate and clarify your services. The point is to organize lots of information in a *few* easy-to-grasp, easy-to-see categories. If you sell retirement plans, for example, a busy page of numbers and dollar values — which realistically reflect your product — may fail to hold the prospect's attention. Make no mistake, he or she needs the facts. But not being the expert you are, a prospect needs the details pulled together in broader categories.

Or, let's say you're a lawyer, accountant or consultant. You sell expert air in its most ethereal form — advice — based on esoteric information. To develop new business ("rainmaking" to most professionals), you create a 10-page brochure describing in minute detail each of your practice areas. But with few pictures or graphic design elements to guide them through the data, it's no surprise that many prospects don't read this very important, very expensive sales tool.

You need to simplify the picture. Package the small details of your service benefits into larger categories, and you'll improve the eyesight of your prospects. You then have numerous explicit and subtle ways to test a closing: "Can you see yourself in this picture?" Or, "What else would you like to see from us?"

Another way to create tangible reminders of service benefits is to provide prospects with third-party evaluations of your work, including testimonials from clients and industry surveys that rank or rate your company. Third-party evaluations give prospects the objective help they need in deciding whether to work with you. At the same time, your reputation as a professional gains critical mass when it's supported by independent parties who have no vested interest in your firm or bias against it.

Use highly visual sales tools to illustrate and clarify your service benefits.

Likewise, you can communicate your service benefits swiftly by relating stories and anecdotes about the client experience. Prospects can put their intellectual arms around such stories and remember the information better. If asked to recite a nursery rhyme or favorite story from childhood, most of us can do so with ease. That's the power of stories versus facts. Contrast the ability to recall stories with the ability to quote a page from a personnel manual, and you'll see why prospects need to hear stories about what the customer experience will be like for them.

Put the prospect in the frame. Most sales require numerous interactions prior to closing. So once you've created a colorful picture of your services at the initial presentation, have the prospect talk to present clients for references. This puts him or her right in the picture frame; the prospect can test-drive your services vicariously through another client's experiences.

Present customers are your best sales tool because they understand the value of your services first hand. To set the stage for these references, ask a number of clients whether they would be willing to receive the calls. Select a variety of clients by size, industry, usage or whatever variables pertain to your market.

Then, contact the present client before each reference call to explain the prospect's need for your services. It's a good idea to arrange a specific time for the call as well. Many reference calls get hung up in a terminal telephone tag between busy people; your help in setting the appointment cuts through this time waster.

A second way to put your prospect in the picture frame is to have him or her visit your offices and meet key staff members. The prospect will want to meet service and support people and, of course, the administrative managers who will bill them and collect invoices. These early introductions smooth the way for a good working relationship that stretches into the future.

Don't worry that your office is not lavish enough to show to prospective customers. When questioned, prospects almost always talk about the importance of meeting key people; the offices, unless they are disorderly, are rarely remarked upon. Prospects do business with people they feel comfortable with. They want to make sure their gut feeling about a service provider's staff corresponds with their intellectual choice. The office visit warms up your sales pitch with faces — the same people who later will service the account, answer the client's questions and fix problems. With so many service providers in competition for the same client, it is people, not office features, that create a sustainable advantage.

This trip to the "service factory," coupled with reference calls, is far more persuasive than any sales presentation, however polished it may be. Why? Because an independent person speaks about your product (the reference) and prospects get to check their comfort level through personal interactions (the visit). They then have objective advice and real people to use in making a decision in your favor.

Animate the picture. At this point, closing the sale should be a natural outgrowth of the conversations you've had with the prospect. Then, you can turn your attention to relationship maintenance, with a focus on documenting, evaluating and reviewing your collective commitments with the customer. Without this maintenance, the client picture stands still. It never takes on a life of its own and fuels the customer loyalty that will make him or her *your* advocate in the marketplace.

Allow the prospect to test-drive your services through a present client's experiences.

Instead, the relationship may deteriorate and eventually require CPR, which means you will spend inordinate amounts of time just returning to "normal." And you may very well lose the client. In that case, you will have to find three more to replace the original customer — a process that is five to six times more expensive than maintaining an existing relationship.

Although much has been written about quality issues, the real quality of client support services usually gets delivered by front-line people — you and your key staffers. The tools of this delivery are time and energy, both of which are in short supply for most professionals. Therefore, the best approach is to take some simple but effective steps to keep present relationships healthy. These include:

- Document by letter or contract your collective commitments: We'll do this, and you, Mr. Client, will do that. By getting these points in writing, you continue to give shape to your expert air and reinforce your trustworthy behavior.
- Establish regular times — say, each quarter — to sit down and review the relationship. Bring both written reports on your work (tangible reminders) and your key people to the account review. Use the time to make any necessary adjustments to your commitments and to resell to the client. You'll add revenue dollars with high profit margins because there is little acquisition cost. And, it's a good place to ask for referrals.
- Make the client a partner in formulating your business strategy. Ask for the client's advice on points such as the following: "How can we do this better? What other services should we add? If you were in my shoes, what other support services would you promote?"
- Make the client your equal by inviting him or her to events you hold, whether they're social or educational. Always ask customers to bring a colleague or friend with them. That way, your client function becomes a fertile selling ground.

Selling expert air requires distinct tactics which, if left undone, will cost you a lot of time and money. So remember to make the sales presentation visual and put the prospect in the picture with client references and office visits. And, most important, actively manage the relationship so that you can reap the rewards of repeat business and references. Profitability springs from customer retention — not sales volume, not market share, and certainly not air alone.

The author is president of The Success Group, New York, a consulting firm that specializes in sales and marketing for professionals.

Chapter Five

Women and Minorities as Rainmakers

by Kathleen Waits[1]
Former Visiting Associate Professor
Albany Law School

BOTH WOMEN AND minority lawyers face special problems in marketing. This chapter addresses those problems and suggests solutions and resources that women and minorities may find helpful in overcoming the rainmaking obstacles they may encounter. The chapter also includes an extensive resource guide to help you tailor your rainmaking plan to your particular situation.

The hurdles to rainmaking encountered by women and minorities can be quite similar, and women lawyers of color naturally carry a double burden. However, the dilemmas faced by women and minorities are different enough that each group will be treated separately.

Women and minority rainmakers should always remember that rainmaking is a challenge to *all* lawyers, regardless of sex, race, or ethnicity. Special panels for women rainmakers have drawn huge crowds at recent ABA meetings, including many white men. Marketing may be less comfortable for white men than many women or minorities may suppose. Women and minority rainmakers have done the whole profession a service by bringing the rainmaking challenge into the open and addressing honestly the joys and pitfalls of marketing.

WOMEN AS RAINMAKERS

Overview

For many women the key issue in approaching rainmaking is this: *Can I be myself and also be a rainmaker?* Many of us imagine the extroverted, glad-handing man as the sole model for rainmaking. Or we may imagine golf and the "ol' boy" network as the only paths to marketing success. Many women ask themselves, "How much must I emulate male models or can I generate business in my own special, female way?"

The best answer to this question is: *Don't reject the male model out of hand, but don't accept it blindly as the only way*. Many of the best women rainmakers have broken out of the mold and have followed different paths to success than men. For example, Roberta Ramo, who is the first woman president of the ABA, came up in the association through the Law Practice Management Section, a route never before followed by the dozens of men who preceded her as ABA president.

Another piece of good news for women who worry that they don't have the "right stuff" for rainmaking: *Being a good lawyer with satisfied clients is the single most important step in being a good rainmaker.*

Some of the ways in which women are raised in our society can be impediments to successful rainmaking. For example, women are strongly discouraged from talking about their successes, and even from feeling pride in their achievements. Studies have shown that even the most accomplished women often attribute their success to luck rather than to their own hard work and talent.

As a woman raised in this society, you may need to ask yourself, Is your hesitancy to make rain and ask for business a result of undue modesty? Do you think you're a good lawyer? If so, then *start telling yourself that you're doing your current and potential clients a favor by informing them about the services you can provide.*

Good rainmakers project competence. It's important to realize that *projecting* competence is different from *being* competent. Of course, you must *be* competent in order to satisfy your clients and develop a good reputation. But many excellent lawyers fail to project competence, and hurt themselves as a result.

There are as many ways of projecting competence as there are successful lawyers. Projecting competence doesn't mean you have to brag; it doesn't even mean being extroverted. Ways to project competence include speaking and writing, inviting clients to group discussions or seminars, keeping clients informed through conversations about your work and new laws affecting their business, writing a newsletter and distributing it to clients. If you think you could do more to project competence, look around for a lawyer who projects competence and whose personality seems similar to your own. Try to emulate that person. If possible, talk to that person about how he or she came to project competence. If you find yourself in a tough situation and your resolve to project competence is flagging, just say to yourself, "For the next five minutes, I'm going to pretend to be X and act as she'd act." By acting confident, you can often become confident.

Be sure to give yourself credit, and to get credit from your firm, for the rainmaking you do. Because women are encouraged in our society to be modest about their achievements, we may be especially reluctant to see ourselves as rainmakers or to take credit for the business we bring in. Many women who are perceived by others as rainmakers don't see themselves that way. Before embarking on new rainmaking efforts, review carefully what you've already done. You may well discover that there are clients you've brought in or gotten new business from and not even realized it. Your review may also point out fruitful avenues for future rainmaking or reveal methods that didn't work.

Social upbringing also explains why *asking for business may be particularly hard for women, especially at first.* Depending on your age, you may have been socialized to wait to be asked out on a date, not to be the person who does the asking. However, many women lawyers, once they find a way of asking for business that's comfortable for them, can at least tolerate it (and many even come to enjoy it). Lorraine Remo, Law Office of Lorraine Remo, Albany, offers this tip about asking for business: "If I have to make a call in which I want to ask for business, I always do it when I'm feeling 'up,' such as the morning after a big victory. It's a lot easier to make that call when I'm feeling good about myself. I also think your chances of success are better when things are going well. You're more attractive to clients when you're optimistic and cheerful than when you're down."

If fear is keeping you from making certain rainmaking efforts, consider reading *Feel the Fear and Do It Anyway* or similar self-help books.[2]

Many lawyers find that it helps them if they have at their command a number of stock phrases that they can use in certain recurring marketing situations. For example, after a client or prospective client raises an issue at a social gathering, you might respond, "It sounds like I might be helpful to you. Can we schedule some time to talk further?" Or, "If you're interested in discussing some alternatives, why don't we set up a time." When representation on a given matter is closed, further work can be sought with, "How else can I be of service to you this year, or in the future, concerning this issue or problem or changes in the laws and regulations affecting your business?" To cross-sell: "My colleague (or I) handles that type of work as well. Let's set up a time to discuss your problem." To obtain referrals: "You probably have colleagues or friends with the same issues. If I can be helpful, please tell them to call me to discuss their problems." Or, "I'd be happy to chair a meeting, or hold a seminar or briefing for your colleagues"; or, "I'd be glad to write for your organization's newsletter."

Finally, as you work to project confidence, to ask clients for business, etc., don't worry that you're a fraud, that you're not really the excellent lawyer that everyone thinks you are. *All* successful people worry that they're frauds who are about to be exposed. Harry Wellington, when he was dean at Yale Law School, would tell the first-year class, "I know that many of you are afraid that here at Yale you're finally going to be discovered to be a fraud; that you're not nearly as smart or capable as everyone thinks." Following a gasp of recognition from the students, Wellington would continue, "Don't worry about it. I'm the *dean* of Yale Law School and I *still* wake up feeling that way every morning."

Special Issues for Women

Entertaining Clients

The golf outing, the big football game, going out for drinks with just the lawyer and the client — entertaining clients in these ways have sometimes been seen as absolute prerequisites for rainmaking. Yet many lawyers, both men and women, are not comfortable with these activities. They don't know how to golf, and don't want to learn; they hate football; going out for drinks with a client seems more like a date than a business meeting. Additionally, women (and sometimes men, too), especially those with families, may not have the time to spend on these activities, or may not want to use their precious free time this way.

Entertaining clients is a perfect example of how women should consider the traditional male model, but should not feel bound by it. Of course, some women participate and enjoy the traditional male-bonding activities. Many women enjoy spectator sports.

However, some women rainmakers focus on business and don't do a lot of entertaining with clients. They establish their expertise through writing, or appearing at seminars and continuing legal education programs. Some clients are a lot more impressed with this kind of work than with an extravagant country club reception. Additionally, some clients — especially those with young children — may also be disinterested in spending their free time away from their families.

If you and your firm do entertain clients, try to find activities that both you and your clients/prospective clients (and also their spouses) enjoy. Recognize that some clients hate football and love ballet.

Consider also events that include families: a family outing at the ballpark, a picnic or pool party where children are included. Some clients may prefer this kind of entertaining.

Try to get your firm to *avoid entertaining at discriminatory clubs or those that are unwelcome to women and minorities*. Some firms and bar associations now have clear policies on these issues. Since 1981, the New York State Bar Association has had a policy stating that association meetings can be held only at places that do not discriminate based on race, national origin, religion, or sex.

To golf or not to golf? Some women lawyers and corporate executives have taken up the game and like it. But if you don't golf and don't want to learn, keep reminding yourself (and others) that there are plenty of fabulously successful male rainmakers who've never held a golf club in their hands.

Appearance

Like it or not, appearance will be scrutinized more carefully for a woman lawyer than for a man. Once again, different lawyers offer different solutions to this issue. Responses may also depend on the type of law you practice. Cristine Cioffi, of Lewis, Kaehler, Bates, Angle, Jones & Cioffi, Schenectady, does estates and trust work. She says that she tries to look at all times like someone who could be entrusted with a $1 million estate. For Cioffi, this means wearing makeup and fairly nice clothes even when running Saturday errands.

On the other hand, Mae D'Agostino, a prominent trial attorney with Maynard, O'Connor, Smith, Catalinotto, & D'Agostino, Albany, is a self-described "bad girl" on the weekends. D'Agostino says she's not prepared to dress up on weekends, so she must do other things during the week to generate business. D'Agostino even sees a benefit in this approach, given her reputation as a tough litigator: "Clients who run into me on the weekends enjoy seeing the other side of me, which hopefully is a little kinder and gentler than I am on the weekdays."

The increased attention devoted to women's appearance may not be all bad news. Some women lawyers feel that their differing appearance can sometimes be an advantage. Many successful women lawyers have abandoned the "dress for success" look and adopted a style that suits them. Because women enjoy a broader latitude in acceptable business clothes than men, this can help a woman stand out from the crowd.

Dealing with Bias in Your Firm and Among Clients

Bias against women is a reality in law firms and among clients. This bias often has an important negative impact on women's careers in private firms, including their ability to attract and retain clients. Despite the huge increase in the number of women graduating from law school, women are not advancing in private law firms at the same rate as men. According to Martha Fay Africa, author of *Darwin's Daughters Hit the Glass Ceiling*, 50 percent of women who enter private practice leave within five years; only 23 percent of women make partner, while 59 percent of men do. The disparity is perhaps greatest in the big firms, where women represent only 8 percent of the partners in the nation's 250 largest firms. Africa's article describes an extensive survey of women lawyers that revealed some of the impediments faced by them, including "male clients who refuse to be represented by female attorneys [and] senior male colleagues [who are] reluctant to support female attorneys for fear of losing important clients." The survey also indicated that nearly all the respondents believe that sexual harassment from clients presents a problem for women lawyers. (A number of the readings in the resource guide at the end of this chapter discuss other barriers encountered by women lawyers.)

Depending on the setting and their own personalities and preferences, *different women take different approaches in dealing with bias*. Decide what works for you. You may want to talk with other women lawyers, especially those whose personalities and practice settings seem similar to your own, about how they've dealt with discrimination.

You may be comfortable with a fairly direct approach, especially if you're already recognized in your firm as a good lawyer and/or rainmaker. Some women lawyers have succeeded in insisting that their firm not hold events at clubs that discriminate. Others have bravely pointed out to senior lawyers, and even clients, situations where they or other women have felt excluded or belittled.

Recognize that you're not alone in confronting bias. In addition to, or instead of, confronting bias directly and individually in their firms, *many women have joined with other women to address and eliminate bias*. For example, the Women's Bar Association of the State of New York vigorously supported a bill, now enacted into law, barring discrimination by large, private clubs whose members' dues and other costs are regularly paid for by non-members (i.e., their firms or businesses).

On the other hand, some women opt for a more subtle approach. A woman partner who is a major rainmaker for her New Jersey firm simply turns over to a senior male associate clients who don't want a woman lawyer. Because of her position, she apparently is confident that she'll receive proper credit for this rainmaking. Women attorneys who are less recognized as rainmakers probably would not find this approach workable for them.

Supporting Others and Getting Support for Yourself

The most consistent advice from all successful rainmakers is: Network, network, network. For women and minorities especially, this often translates to: Look for mentors and be a mentor.

Obviously, you should look for mentors and be a mentor within your firm. However, many women, especially those who are in firms with only one or two women lawyers, may find intrafirm mentoring opportunities limited. Even those who get mentoring within their firms should want and need to network in a larger sphere.

As will be discussed below, women lawyers have sometimes benefited greatly from men as mentors. Traditional male-dominated bar and business associations can also help women generate business. Nevertheless, many women lawyers find women's groups indispensable to their networking and rainmaking.

You should strongly consider becoming involved in women's bar associations on the national, state, or local level. Many of the most successful women rainmakers have made invaluable contacts and received many referrals through these organizations. Additionally, women's bar groups can be a tremendous resource for brainstorming and venting.

Traditional bar groups are also giving more attention to women's issues. Increasingly, women are becoming powerful in groups like the New York State Bar Association and the ABA. Consider becoming involved in groups like the ABA's Women Rainmakers Interest Group or the NYSBA's Committee on Women in the Law, especially its Subcommittee on Women in the Profession.

Remember to not only seek out mentors but to be a mentor. Make time to talk to those who seek out your advice and counsel, especially other women who are just getting started. This a duty you owe to the profession. It can also pay off in the long run. Practically everyone who takes mentoring seriously reports getting referrals or recommendations from someone they mentored.

Rainmakers of all types recommend involvement in social action and community organizations as being important to business development. Not only will you feel good about using your personal and legal skills to achieve a worthwhile goal, you will meet like-minded people, many of whom may become clients or sources for referrals. Women's bar groups, regular bar groups, other women's organizations, political organizations, and community groups are all ways of getting involved.

Don't be afraid to stand up for what you believe in, even on controversial issues. Lawyers in America are expected to be opinion leaders and activists. Many women lawyers, including some major rainmakers, have, for example, been visible in political campaigns.

Unless your work comes largely from other attorneys, you will probably want most of your networking to involve non-lawyers. You should consider both traditional and women-oriented business groups. Most chambers of commerce now have women's business groups; consider getting involved. Women's networks can be a tremendous source of referrals; most women lawyers and businesspeople are eager to help other women.

If your business depends on referrals from lawyers outside your firm, be sure not to "poach" on their clients. Leslie E. Stein practices domestic relations law at the large Albany firm of McNamee, Lochner, Titus & Williams. She often gets referrals from other lawyers of high-level business executives with family law problems. Stein says, "I don't try to 'cross-sell' with these clients. I don't make any effort to bring their corporate business into my firm. If I did, word would quickly get around and no one would refer their clients to me for matrimonial work. Occasionally these clients, on their own, decide to switch to our firm, but lawyers in other firms know that I can be trusted not to steal their clients."

Look carefully at the spouses of clients. Treat them like the interesting, intelligent people they are. Many will be in the work force themselves and can be helpful in their own rights as referral sources or through their spouses. And don't assume that traditional stay-at-home wives are hostile or indifferent to your success; many are very supportive of professional women.

More generally, *don't make assumptions about who's supportive and who's not*. This applies especially in looking for mentors. In *The Last Frontier: Women Lawyers as Rainmakers*, C. Beth DunCombe, a black woman partner in a large Detroit firm, talks about her mentor, an elderly white male partner who was considered "kind of a grump." Yet he had no problem referring his clients to DunCombe and encouraging them to look upon her as their lawyer. DunCombe comments, "From this relationship I learned that both male and female mentors are welcome in my life. You can learn from a lot of people and a lot of people can help you."

The Success of Being Yourself

Can there be marketing advantages to being a woman? Some successful women rainmakers think so. Martha Barnett, who chairs the ABA House of Delegates, says in *The Last Frontier: Women Lawyers as Rainmakers*, "Women are naturals at rainmaking. We are listeners, we are counselors, we are aggressive, but we are *not* like men. I have found that clients appreciate that aspect of what they get from women."

While women's greater emotional openness is generally a blessing, discretion is also important. Probably because they are often burdened with a disproportionate share of family responsibilities, women may be more likely than men to talk openly about how busy and overwhelmed they feel. This is a mistake if done with clients, prospective clients, or potential referral sources. The natural, if unspoken, reaction to such statements is, "Gee, it sounds as if she couldn't handle any more business. Even though I think she's a great lawyer, I guess I should take my business elsewhere." Rainmakers always convey the attitude, "I'm busy, but never too busy to take on appropriate new work and clients. Your business [or referral] is always welcome." Obviously, women lawyers sometimes need to discuss their feelings about time pressure and family burdens, but they need to select appropriate settings to do so.

Another advantage women may have is that they are comfortable being "cross-sellers" and "team players." Women enjoy generating business for other lawyers in their firm, or being part of a team that helps acquire a new client or expand business with an existing one. These are keys to rainmaking success that many men could learn from. Indeed, as is discussed elsewhere in this book, cross-selling, referrals, and new work from existing clients are absolutely critical to profitable marketing.

Finally, *some clients may be looking for a woman lawyer.* Women-owned small businesses are one of the fastest growing segments of the American economy, and many women entrepreneurs want to use and support women professionals. That's why women's chamber of commerce groups can be so important to women lawyers' rainmaking. Note, however, that many women in business focus their own networking on *men's* groups because these groups have more money and wider contacts. Find out where the women businesspeople are and put yourself in a position to meet them.

Minorities as Rainmakers[3]

Obstacles

Lawyers who belong to racial and ethnic minorities probably face even greater marketing challenges than white women. Minorities are seriously underrepresented among lawyers generally and especially in the most prestigious and lucrative parts of the profession. Although minorities represent close to one-quarter of the American population, African-Americans represent only 3.2 percent of the nation's lawyers and Hispanics represent only 2.7 percent. Of the partners in the nation's 250 largest law firms, less than 1 percent are black.[4]

Minority lawyers, even those who have attended the most prestigious colleges and law schools, often lack long-standing connections to powerful, wealthy people and to the traditional power structure of American business. Minority lawyers are unlikely to be members of social institutions (country clubs, etc.) that provide important rainmaking connections.

Even worse, many clients and potential clients may assume that minority lawyers are not as qualified, intelligent, or competent as their white counterparts. Clients may feel that minority lawyers do not "deserve" to be where they are and that their achievements reflect unfair affirmative action rather than minority lawyers' merits. These assumptions are rarely articulated directly, but can have a pervasive effect on a minority lawyer's ability to generate business and prove worthy of a client's trust and confidence.

The discomfort of some clients with minority attorneys may be even greater than their discomfort with white women lawyers. Obviously, women attorneys of color are in the worst position in terms of being "odd" and "different" from their clients. The 1994 report of the ABA's Multicultural Women Attorneys Network, *The Burdens of Both, The Privileges of Neither,* describes the many obstacles faced by multicultural women attorneys. The report notes that the special problems of women attorneys of color are often ignored by the majority bar associations and by the women and minority bars. Further, many multicultural women attorneys feel they are forced to choose between their race or ethnicity and their gender. See also Pinder, *When Will Black Women Lawyers Slay the Two-Headed Dragon; Racism and Gender Bias?*, for an eloquent discussion of the indignities faced daily by black women attorneys. These include being mistaken, even when elegantly dressed, for janitorial staff or criminal defendants; being treated suspiciously by receptionists when entering a business or law firm; being treated as an expert on all issues remotely related to race or sex but as having nothing to offer on any other topic.

Because there are so few senior, experienced minority lawyers, lack of role models and mentors is a serious problem for minority lawyers who are just starting in practice and in rainmaking.

Minority lawyers in large firms may face particular frustration as rainmakers and in getting credit for the rainmaking they do. McHugh, *Minority Lawyers Are Rainmakers Despite Odds: Survey* reports on the findings of a survey conducted of minority partners in large (25+ lawyers) law firms. Sixty percent of the respondents thought that they actually brought in as much business as their white partners, but were generally not given credit for the rainmaking they did. They further reported that most of their rainmaking was with non-minority clients, since in their experience many minority individuals and companies cannot afford the fees charged by large law firms. If access to corporate decision makers seems foreclosed by the structure of a large firm, minorities in large firms may want to consider the suggestion made by Otis in *Wringing the Clouds Dry: The Minority Attorney's Guide to Rainmaking*. Otis advises minorities in large firms to focus on excelling as lawyers and developing specialized expertise.

Some minority lawyers in small firms, generally out of frustration with discouraging attempts to generate legal business in the white community, may decide to look primarily to their own minority community for business. Though concentrating on the minority community has worked for some lawyers, for others it results in a client base that's too limited. Minorities may need to look at innovative marketing approaches. Consider, for example, the strategy used by Renaye B. Cuyler, Gorayeb & Cuyler, New York City, to build her firm from three lawyers when it opened in 1986 to 13 lawyers in 1994. While most personal injury firms specialize in either plaintiffs' or defendants' work, Cuyler's firm does both. The firm's plaintiffs' representation is mostly from the African-American community, while its representation of insurance company defendants has naturally required the firm to market to a predominantly white audience. In approaching corporate clients, Cuyler emphasizes the cost-effectiveness of using her relatively small firm.

Positive Suggestions

If, as a minority lawyer, you feel that you're being treated as not "up to snuff," look for ways to counter that perception. For example, Renaye Cuyler makes a point of mentioning in conversations when her credentials are being questioned by white clients that she attended law school on an *academic* scholarship, not one given exclusively to minority students. On the need for minority lawyers to overcome the assumption that they are not competent and intelligent, Cuyler comments, "I just deal with it and move on."

Minority lawyers also report facing particularly strong assumptions that their writing skills are not good. The experienced minority lawyers interviewed by Suzanne Baer and Londell McMillan for the "Career Opportunities for Minorities" chapter in *Changing Jobs: A Handbook for Lawyers in the 1990s* advised, "Build an impressive writing portfolio." This can be done by "remember[ing] writers are made, not born." Suggestions on writing opportunities include: "Get on a bar association committee and write a report. Write an article or even a letter to the editor and get it published. Write a long letter to a judge about a trial issue that interests you . . . get on CLE panels, and keep a file of speeches." Other ideas: write for a trade journal or newspaper and send copies of your article to interested current and prospective clients.

As with white women, networking and visibility are critical to the success of minority rainmakers. Successful minority lawyers urge their colleagues to be visible in various professional, political, social, and social service organizations, serving both minority and white communities. Particularly helpful (and rewarding both personally and professionally) may be organizations and activities that build bridges between minority and white communities.

Another common piece of advice: *link with other minority attorneys in state, local, national minority bar groups and in minority "caucuses" within traditional bar associations.* These can be important sources of moral support as well as networking and providing referrals. The experienced minority lawyers interviewed by Baer and McMillan recommend: "Network with experienced minority lawyers because you need those who have been through it to tell you how they made it."

These successful minority lawyers also told Baer and McMillan that new lawyers should look for mentors and role models wherever they may arise. They said, "When you start out in law practice, make friends with everybody. Everyone can help you." And, "The best way to learn what to do is to watch people who excel at what you want to do."

Many minority attorneys use their contacts with government lawyers as a major part of their rainmaking efforts. A disproportionate number of minority and women lawyers and other professionals are employed by government at all levels. A minority lawyer in private practice should consider networking with government lawyers and looking for ways in which they may be sources for referrals and government contracting-out of legal services.

Time may be on the side of minority rainmakers. American society is changing. More and more of the workforce and consumers will be people of minority backgrounds. This may create new opportunities for minority lawyers. Minority lawyers should identify businesses (both large and small) and contracting-out government agencies that are interested in hiring minority lawyers and law firms.

The National Bar Association, the ABA, and the New York State Bar Association have all been involved in projects designed to increase minority lawyers' access to corporate business, such as the ABA's Minority Counsel Demonstration Program and the NYSBA's Minority Counsel Project. These projects are designed to introduce corporations to minority lawyers and minority-owned law firms that can provide corporations with high-quality, cost-effective representation. (To learn more about these programs, see contacts listed in the resource guide at the end of this chapter.)

These projects are critical because they provide minority lawyers with access to potential clients. Of course, like all lawyers, you must still convince the client of the value of your services, and satisfy your clients once they hire you. But these projects at least give minority lawyers someone to contact, a name to call, in order to begin their marketing efforts.

Some local bar associations, in cooperation with the New York State Bar Association, are also engaged in efforts to increase the hiring and retention of minority lawyers in private firms, usually medium to large firms. One such program operating in the Buffalo area is Attorney Access, a now-independent organization that began as a joint project of the Bar Association of Erie County and the Minority Bar Association of Western New York. Check your local bar associations (both majority and minority) and the NYSBA to participate in — or to initiate — similar programs in your area.

Certain large companies (GM and IBM have been especially prominent) have hired and retained minority lawyers for their in-house staff. They are also putting pressure on their outside law firms to hire more minority lawyers, and are providing an increasing amount of their business to minority-owned firms. These new initiatives may provide leverage for minorities to insist on becoming part of their firm's marketing team.

The motives of these companies are not necessarily altruistic. Instead, they recognize that since the consumers of their products are increasingly diverse, those consumers will more and more demand that corporations reflect that diversity. Further, American businesses will need a diverse workforce to correctly understand a diverse population's needs.

Finally, an increasing amount of international legal business will come from non-European countries in Africa, Asia, and South America. Minority lawyers may wish to encourage the development of this business and see about getting in on the ground floor. Minority lawyers who are multilingual can exploit this talent to develop business from the "global village."

A Final Word for Women, Minority, and *All* Rainmakers — Keep Plugging

Life is still not easy for women and minority lawyers. However, the secret for *all* rainmakers is: *keep plugging*. As individuals and as a society, we have a long way to go, but we have also come far. Ten years ago, the special rainmaking challenges for women and minority lawyers were barely being discussed. As the resource guide below indicates, today there are a large number of organizations, books, articles and videos that are addressing these concerns. Consider which ones might help you in developing your marketing strategies. Remember always that marketing is an ongoing process. Periodically, you will need to reevaluate your marketing plan. This means that marketing approaches that don't make sense for you today may be just the thing a year from now. You will therefore want to come back to this chapter, and especially the resource materials, as you move along the rainmaker's path.

Good luck!

Endnotes

1. I would like to thank the following people, all of whom gave generously of their time and expertise in helping me produce this chapter: Cristine Cioffi of Lewis, Kaehler, Bates, Angle, Jones & Cioffi, Schenectady; Renaye Cuyler of Gorayeb & Cuyler, New York City; Mae D'Agostino of Maynard, O'Connor, Smith, Catalinotto, & D'Agostino, Albany; Patsy Engelhard, ABA Commission on Women in the Profession; Christine Filip of The Success Group, New York City; L. Beth Krueger, Director of Administrative Services, New York State Bar Association; Sandra L. Mans, Assistant Dean for Career Planning, Albany Law School; Lorraine Remo of the Law Office of Lorraine Remo, Albany; and Leslie Stein of McNamee, Lochner, Titus & Williams, Albany.

2. Use of self-help books can be a tricky business, especially for women. A good guideline: If a particular self-help book doesn't work for you or is just making you feel bad about yourself, *toss it*. Of course, self-examination and self-improvement are often painful. But many self-help books, especially many geared specifically toward women, focus on your weaknesses rather than your strengths. A good self-help book makes you say, "This may be tough, but I can do it!" Also, be wary of any book that says, "There is only one way to do this." People are different; what works for one person may be all wrong for another. Have confidence in yourself as a unique individual; if your gut tells you that a particular piece of advice is wrong for you, trust your gut.

3. As a white woman, I feel somewhat uncomfortable giving advice to minority rainmakers. I am especially grateful to Renaye Cuyler, Gorayeb & Cuyler, New York City, for sharing her insights into these issues.

4. Statistics taken from D'Alemberte, *Racial Injustice and American Justice*, ABA Journal, August 1992, p. 58 and Johnson, *Defending the Use of Quotas in Affirmative Action: Attacking Racism in the Nineties*, 1992 U. Ill. L. Rev. 1043, 1054-55. *See also* Jensen, *Minorities Didn't Share in Firm Growth*, Nat'l L.J., Feb. 19, 1990, p. 1.

RESOURCE GUIDE

Women as Rainmakers

ORGANIZATIONS

American Bar Association
750 North Lake Shore Drive
Chicago, IL 60611
(312) 988-5000

Of particular interest: Committee on Women in the Profession
(312) 988-5676

Multicultural Women Attorneys Network — a joint project of the ABA Committee on Women in the Profession and the ABA Commission on Opportunities for Minorities in the Profession
(312) 988-5676

Women Rainmakers Interest Group, ABA Law Practice Management Section
(312) 988-5619

Association of Black Women Attorneys
c/o Adrienne Williams
134 West 32nd Street, Suite 602
New York, NY 10001
(718) 935-3377

New York State Bar Association
One Elk Street
Albany, NY 12207
(518) 463-3200

Of particular interest: Committee on Women in the Law, and its Subcommittee on Participation of Women in the Profession

Women's Bar Association of the State of New York (WBASNY)
245 Fifth Avenue, Suite 2103
New York, NY 10016
(212) 889-7813

Chapters are located in the Bronx, Brooklyn, Buffalo, Capital District (Albany), Rochester, Manhattan, Mid-Hudson (Poughkeepsie), Nassau County, Orange and Sullivan Counties, Queens, Rockland County, Staten Island, Suffolk County and Westchester County. Contact WBASNY headquarters for chapter addresses and contact names.

PUBLICATIONS AND VIDEOS AVAILABLE FROM THE ABA

Order from: ABA Order Fulfillment Department
750 North Lake Shore Drive
Chicago, IL 60611
(312) 988-5522
(312) 988-5568 (fax)

Prices below are without shipping and handling; Visa and MasterCard accepted for charge by phone.

The Burdens of Both, The Privileges of Neither, Multicultural Women Attorneys Network (1994), $10.00.

The Last Frontier: Women Lawyers as Rainmakers. [Product #511-0314; $14.95, plus shipping and handling; $9.95 for Law Practice Management section members.]

Women Rainmakers: Strategies for Effective Networking [video; 50 min.]. [Product #511-0313; $30; $19.95 for Women Rainmakers Interest Group members.]

Women Rainmakers' Marketing Tips [$19.95].

Pitulla, *The Persistence of Bias in the Legal Profession*, The Professional Lawyer, 1993 Symposium Issue, ABA Center for Professional Responsibility. Includes bibliography of reports and articles on discrimination against women and minorities in the profession.

OTHER PUBLICATIONS

Bowing to New Rules: Lawyers Confront Gender Bias, The Compleat Lawyer, Summer 1994 (several articles devoted to women rainmakers and other gender bias issues in the legal profession).

Making It Pour: How Women Attorneys Can Attract and Keep Clients, available for $1.00 from Joint Task Force on Gender Fairness, Ohio State Bar Association, 1700 Lake Shore Drive, Columbus, Ohio 43204.

Working Paper of the Ninth Circuit Gender Bias Task Force, Report of the Advisory Committee on Bankruptcy, prepared by Hon. Lisa Hill Fenning, United States Bankruptcy Judge, Central District of California, April, 1993, reprinted in Practising Law Institute, Commercial Law and Practice Course Handbook Series, Advanced Bankruptcy Workshop 1994, PLI Order No. A4-4443 (Feb. 1994)

Africa, Martha Fay. *Darwin's Daughters Hit the Glass Ceiling*, Law Practice Management Magazine, September 1993, p. 18.

Bean, *Women Who Make Rain Without Thunder*, N.J.L.J., August 9, 1993, p. 4.

Farber, *Women as Rainmakers — A Personal Perspective*, Law Practice Management, July/August 1994, p. 27 (whole issue devoted to rainmaking, including articles entitled *How to Ask for Business* and *Young Lawyer Rainmakers*).

Smith, *Female Litigators Eye the New Frontier*, Of Counsel, March 15, 1993, p. 2.

Pinder, *When Will Black Women Lawyers Slay the Two-Headed Dragon: Racism and Gender Bias?*, 20 Pepperdine L. Rev. 1053 (1993).

GENERAL INTEREST BOOKS

Jeffers, *Feel the Fear and Do It Anyway* (Fawcett Columbine, 1987).

RoAne, *How to Work a Room: A Guide to Successfully Managing the Mingling* (Shapolsky Publishers, 1988).

RoAne, *The Secrets of Savvy Networking: How to Make the Best Connections for Business and Personal Success* (Warner Books, 1993). A good follow-up to *How to Work a Room*.

Minorities as Rainmakers

ORGANIZATIONS

American Bar Association
750 North Lake Shore Drive
Chicago, IL 60611
(312) 988-5000

Of particular interest: Commission on Opportunities for Minorities in the Profession
(312) 988-5638

Minority Counsel Demonstration Program
(312) 988-5667

Multicultural Women Attorneys Network
[See women rainmakers' resource guide for information.]

American Indian Bar Association
c/o Tricia Tingle
144-B East San Antonio Street
San Marcos, TX 78666

Association of Black Women Attorneys, Inc.
[See women rainmakers' resource guide for information.]

Attorney Access
601 Convention Tower
43 Court Street
Buffalo, NY 14202
(716) 842-6466

National Asian Pacific American Bar Association
c/o Brian A. Sun
O'Neil & Lysaght
100 Wilshire Blvd., Suite 700
Santa Monica, CA 90401

Hispanic National Bar Association
c/o Wilfredo Caraballo
Seton Hall Law School
One Newark Center
Newark, NJ 07102

National Bar Association
c/o Paulette Brown
Brown & Childress
337 South Harrison Street
East Orange, NJ 07018

New York State Bar Association
One Elk Street
Albany, NY 12207
(518) 463-3200

Of particular interest: Committee on Minorities in the Profession
Minority Counsel Project

PUBLICATIONS AND VIDEOS AVAILABLE FROM THE ABA

Changing Jobs: A Handbook for Lawyers in the 1990s (McNeil, ed. 1994), especially chapter by Suzanne Baer and Londell McMillan, "Career Opportunities for Minorities."

The Burdens of Both, The Privileges of Neither, Multicultural Women Attorneys Network (1994). (See women rainmakers' resource guide for ordering information.)

The Last Frontier: Women Lawyers as Rainmakers — especially remarks by C. Beth DunCombe, black female partner in large Detroit law firm. (See women rainmakers' resource guide for ordering information.)

OTHER PUBLICATIONS

George, *The Economic Unification of Europe and Independent African Nations: Progress or Regression*, Nat'l Bar Assoc. Magazine, May 1991, p. 17.

Keeva, *Unequal Partners: It's Tough at the Top for Minority Lawyers*, ABA Journal, February, 1993, p. 50.

McHugh, *Minority Lawyers Are Rainmakers Despite Odds: Survey*, Chicago Daily Law Bulletin, March 3, 1994, p. 1.

Otis, *Wringing the Clouds Dry: The Minority Attorney's Guide to Rainmaking*, New Jersey Lawyer, November/December, 1992, p. 32.

Pinder, *When Will Black Women Lawyers Slay the Two-Headed Dragon; Racism and Gender Bias?*, 20 Pepperdine L. Rev. 1053 (1993).

Rossheim, *Corporations' Efforts to Attract Minorities Intensify, Increasing Pressure on Law Firms*, Lawyer Hiring & Training Report, November, 1992, p. 1.

GENERAL INTEREST BOOKS

See list in women rainmakers' resource guide, above.

Chapter Six

How Computers Support Marketing

by

Stephen P. Gallagher

J. Richardson Lippert, II

Computers and Marketing

by Stephen P. Gallagher

DRAMATIC ENVIRONMENTAL CHANGE is taking place in the legal marketplace, and it is becoming increasingly important for lawyers to explore ways to run their practices more efficiently and cost-effectively. Let's start our discussion about computers and marketing by reflecting on the changes that are driving the legal marketplace.

Imagine a court with no paper, no mail, and no copy machine, where documents are filed and linked electronically to related statutory references and case decisions. Imagine a court like the Midtown Manhattan Community Court that uses workflow software, courtwide public display systems, and an Electronic Judicial Desktop which displays comprehensive criminal information pertaining to arrests, criminal record, charge, complaint, and plea agreement status. Imagine a court like the Maricopa County Superior Court in Phoenix, Arizona, that has established a do-it-yourself "Justice Depot" in the courthouse, where clerks show people how to prepare forms and tell them where and when to file them. In addition, imagine that this same court has installed 140 "QuickCourt" computers, where litigants can punch in their legal problems and, in seconds, receive directions on how to proceed with their cases.

As the profession continues to reshape itself, to find new ways to deliver services that provide access to people with everyday legal problems, it is hard to imagine practitioners succeeding without effective use of the new technology to meet these challenges. The American Bar Association's Legal Technology Resource Center conducted a survey of Automation in Smaller Law Firms to explore the state of technology in the profession, and they reported that, currently, 83 percent of respondents use PCs (terminals) in their law practice. Last year, according to the Software Publishing Association, 62 percent of the personal computers bought for home use included a modem. As of mid-1994, the lawyers' special interest group (SIG) on CompuServe numbered 72,480 members, making it the largest interest group on any Bulletin Board Service, averaging 500 to 600 messages per day.

The nature of all service industries is fundamentally changing, so keep in mind that "your competition" is much broader than previously imagined. In such industries as banking, financial services, health care, and law, widespread access to high technology tools and increasingly convenient communications and information technology services are now being offered to consumers around the world and around the clock. Just as "doc-in-a-box" software programs and on-line databases and support groups are enabling individuals to manage their own health in ways that until recently were unimaginable, on-line services are increasingly allowing attorneys to respond to the public's real need for greater legal access at a reasonable cost.

Today, mobile computers and communications software are changing the way your competition is working. Whether it is a personal digital assistant that slips into a jacket pocket or compact notebook computers that perform like desktop machines, these computers on-the-go are dramatically changing how you and your clients work. As we discuss how computers might help your marketing efforts, let's take a look at an innovative real estate attorney, who now visits prospective buyers in the comfort of their homes. Using a number of on-line services to do title searches, as well as provide clients with information on local schools, neighborhoods, housing prices and patterns, crime statistics, and other information real estate agents do not normally provide, this sole practitioner has attracted quite a following of business leads.

As in the case of our real estate attorney, this individual's law practice is changing as a direct result of emerging technologies. There are a number of inexpensive conveyancing software programs that are affecting the value of document production for a real estate transaction. The attorney in our example has decided that it is the on-line access to demographic information that will provide individuals and small businesses with the critical information needed to make informed decisions. In gaining a competitive advantage, our real estate attorney needs to create marketing opportunities for her *new business*.

It is certainly possible to practice law today without using computers, but according to Jay G. Foonberg, Esq., author of the American Bar Association's number-one best-seller, *How to Start and Build a Law Practice*, "Computers will not replace lawyers, but lawyers with computers will replace lawyers without computers." Five years from now, the ethics of practicing law without computers won't even be a question.

Look Before You Leap

Computers can be powerful tools in the marketing of legal services, but it can be extremely frustrating to get started. If you have no experience with computers, I would suggest that before purchasing anything, you start talking with colleagues and friends who are more comfortable with technology. As you accumulate suggestions and ideas from your friends, take the time to attend continuing legal education (CLE) programs that demonstrate how computers are being used in specific areas of practice.

Begin reading anything you can get your hands on that relates to how lawyers are using computers. Once you have found a friend whose practice is similar to that of your own, and you are comfortable with the way the individual handles her or his files, you will need to find out more detailed information about this individual's computer system. You will need to acquire a working knowledge of computers to ask the right questions. This cannot be done overnight, so you should devote some time each week to getting started.

You can start your basic research by subscribing to any of a number of newsletters and computer magazines that target the legal profession. High on my list of publications is *Law Office Computing,* which is published six times a year by James Publication, Inc. of Costa Mesa, California. This magazine has a good mix of informative articles from practitioners who are using computers, software reviews that are helpful when you are shopping for specific types of software, and general updates about new products and emerging technologies. This magazine should be passed around the office before finding its final resting place in the client reception area.

Another invaluable publication is *The Lawyer's PC,* which is published twice a month by Shepard's/McGraw-Hill, Inc. This newsletter contains a wealth of practical tips and ideas from practitioners and consultants who have been working with computers for many years. You want to keep past issues of *The Lawyer's PC* in the firm library because, when you begin exploring new software applications, you will in all likelihood find that someone has written about the application in past editions of this publication. If you cannot find any reference to the software or application, you should proceed with caution. Another good reason to examine *The Lawyer's PC* is its annual Software Review. This is an excellent research tool when you decide to upgrade your system.

Other types of newsletters and magazines that should prove to be of value to you are publications such as *Leader's Legal Tech Newsletter*, published by Leader Publications. This particular newsletter takes a more in-depth look at how new technologies are impacting the delivery of legal services. This is probably not the first computer newsletter I would recommend for beginners, but as you mature in your utilization of computers, *Leader's Legal Tech Newsletter* will keep you well informed as to the future direction of the industry.

Finally, many software vendors produce their own newsletters and magazines, which should not be ignored. One good example is WordPerfect Corporation's *WordPerfect for Windows Magazine*. While some of the articles in these publications can be scanned and quickly discarded, others, depending on your specific areas of interest, might prove to be very much on point.

Personal Information Managers (PIMs)

After you have completed your preliminary research into appropriate software, and you have decided to purchase a computer, the software you choose to use could greatly enhance your marketing efforts. Most firms buy computers to improve document production and time and billing processes. This will continue to be the appropriate place to begin; however, for very little additional cost, the computer can become a very powerful tool to help you manage your client information as well as expand services.

Since most lawyers spend much time getting organized — sorting documents, setting appointments, making phone calls, etc. — I would recommend that you consider buying an inexpensive software program that can handle calendaring and scheduling, list creation and management, Rolodex, notepad, and possibly telephone dialing. Today, there are a number of Personal Information Managers (PIMs) that can tackle the most difficult tasks of getting you organized, and these programs are fun to use.

Most people who use PIMs have tried several different programs, so personal preference weighs heavily in selecting software. As a marketing tool PIMs can be quite powerful, because these systems are based on a contact-related structure. All information is connected to a specific person or organization, and many of these systems integrate word processing capabilities with mail-merge features. Contact manager and case management software are very similar to PIM software, and you might want to explore these types of programs.

Our real estate attorney who is using the laptop computer and on-line service to access the demographic databases also uses PIMs software to enable her to follow the status of all contacts she has made. The PIM software allows the attorney to easily track all events, appointments, reminders, things-to-do, and other items on the calendar. At the time the attorney meets a potential client, she immediately enters the name, address, and whatever other relevant information she has into the PIMs software. This initial record is then tickled for action; as a general rule, everyone in the database is contacted every three months. It is important to note that the contact list is much broader than the real estate attorney's client list.

The PIMs software allows you to maintain lists in a variety of ways. You might want to track individuals who have moved to the area from out-of-state. The entire list of contacts might be interested in your quarterly newsletter, while our real estate attorney was particularly interested in tracking females who run their own businesses. After a six-month period of time from the original date of contact, our real estate attorney made it a practice of calling at least two non-client contacts a day. As busy as she was, she set aside time each day to make these calls. The purpose was to follow up on her initial contact of months earlier. She enjoyed these calls and found that, although they were unsolicited, they were well received.

After every telephone contact, the real estate attorney is able to use the point-and-click interface to the word-processing software to easily tailor a short letter to each contact. Personal notes from the most recent telephone conversation were added to create a new record and the file is again tickled for follow-up in three to six months. On a personal note, I use my PIM software to help avoid embarrassment — when the contact that I made several months ago calls me for the first time. If the telephone receptionist announces a caller that I cannot place, I immediately type the first several characters of the individual's name to see if I have a match in the database. Many times this has given me enough information about the contact to recall our previous conversation.

Reach Out and Touch Someone

The mobile office can bring you a new level of efficiency, and those who are currently working in that new environment can clearly accumulate and share data faster and with more ease than if using traditional methods. *Computer Reseller News* recently projected the worldwide mobile computing market will reach $69.6 billion by 1999, proceeded by annual sales increases at a compound rate of 36.7 percent throughout the '90s.

There is a wealth of commercially produced digests to court reports, practice materials, and updating services, as well as secondary legal sources such as texts, treatises, encyclopedias, and legal periodicals that are available through on-line legal database services. Additionally, we are seeing lawyers — like our real estate practitioner — using computers to electronically link to office-based desktop PCs, local-area networks and commercial bulletin board services (BBSs). The demographic databases accessed for the prospective home owners are found on CompuServe Information Services.

The New York State Bar Association, the largest voluntary bar association in the nation, provides lawyers in New York State with a package of electronic services that consists of a series of notice boards for current information, a full electronic mail and document exchange system, and gateways to outside databases and services of relevance to lawyers. Rather than being structured as an on-line database, the New York State Bar Association network ("NYLaw/Net") is a communications facility to provide lawyers access to the numerous interconnected electronic services designed to meet the information needs of the New York legal community. By using the electronic network, practitioners will be able to adopt new and different ways of providing services more rapidly *and* cost-effectively — an advantage with increasingly greater impact as state and local governments make available a broader range of public information.

Through any of the popular on-line services, lawyers are able to instantly research non-legal, specific databases to better service clients. Anyone can access the numerous corporate databases and keep current on news items of interest to clients no matter where you are or what time it is. The three major on-line services — America Online, CompuServe and Prodigy — currently claim nearly 5 million subscribers, and close to another 20 million people can be reached through the Internet, the network of networks which is the nearest thing we have to the information superhighway. The information available through the Internet is expected to continue to grow at an alarming rate, and without mobile technology and electronic communications, it is highly unlikely that you will be able to continue to provide quality legal services at a competitive rate.

Since concern and responsibility for marketing should permeate all areas of the enterprise, innovative adjustments to your business will create new marketing opportunities. The challenge is to begin to explore how computers can help us adopt new and different ways of providing services more rapidly and more cost-effectively. Marketing is so basic to the business you are in that computerization is sure to present you with marketing tools and techniques to better manage these new opportunities.

Bibliography

Books and Magazines

Law Office Computing, published by James Publishing, Inc., Costa Mesa, CA

The Lawyer's PC, published by Shepard's/McGraw-Hill, Inc., Colorado Springs, CO

Leader's Legal Tech Newsletter, published by Leader Publications, a Division of New York Law Publication, New York, NY

WordPerfect for Windows Magazine, published by WordPerfect, Orem, UT

Information Management Software

1stAct!, Symantec Corporation, Cupertino, CA

ABACUS Law — Calendaring & Case Management System, ABACUS Data Systems, Inc., San Diego, CA

Ecco Professional, Arabesque Software, Inc.

Jr. Partner, Millennium Software Ltd., Conshohocken, PA

Lotus Organizer, Lotus Development Corp.

On-line Services

America Online, (800) 827-6364

CompuServe Information Services, (800) 848-8199

Prodigy, (800) 776-3449

Computer Usage in the Solo/Small Firm

by J. Richardson Lippert, II

Lawyering On-line — A Day in the Life

AS SHE WAS driving to her office, Sara recalled the dilemma that she and Erica, her partner, had faced a few years ago. Their practice in a rural community had finite limits in terms of time and financial resources. The nearest comprehensive law library is more than an hour's drive away and the need for information — both legal and factual — led them to explore the possibility of using computers.

Though they'd used computers in their office for word processing and some billing and accounting chores, that was the extent of it. They made a commitment to buy a modem and determine the usefulness of a computer to communicate and obtain information. Neither of them had gained computer literacy through training, and the first few months were frustrating. The office subscribed to a commercial service and then suddenly a new world — one that neither Sara nor Erica realized existed — unfolded before their eyes.

They experimented with e-mail and the bulletin boards. One useful bulletin board was devoted to the subject of the law. While the two rural practitioners were the only ones in the county to use a computer to communicate in such a manner, they soon discovered that there were other New York State lawyers and several from other states ready to greet them. It seemed that one contact led to another and the benefits of using this new medium of communication more than justified the time spent climbing the learning curve.

Sara arrived at her office shortly after 7:30 a.m. She was due in court at 10 a.m. and wanted to do a last-minute update of her research on the motion to be argued. She also needed to check her correspondence and assign tasks to the staff of two who would be arriving in about an hour.

Erica would be returning from vacation at week's end. Covering her partner's caseload as well as her own was forcing Sara to spend long days and evenings in the office and on her laptop at home.

The motion had first priority. Sara flipped the switch on her computer and modem and jotted a few notes to herself while the computer booted up. She hadn't had a chance to check recent decisions of the Court of Appeals in three or four days and wanted to leave no stone unturned in the final preparation for her motion. As soon as she logged on to the Court of Appeals computer, she learned that the last decisions were handed down yesterday. After quickly checking the directory of decisions, Sara discovered that the court had reported decisions last Thursday and yesterday.

While her computer downloaded the decisions for both days, Sara finished jotting notes to update Erica on a few matters of concern. She logged off the Court of Appeals computer and began to skim the decisions on her monitor. Nothing relevant in Thursday's decisions; what about yesterday's? Suddenly Sara paused and backed up to the beginning of *People v. Bolden*. She had been focusing on the text of the cases, not the titles.

"Oh my God!" she exclaimed out loud, no one hearing her excitement. Without reading the full case, she knew it was on point as she printed a hard copy. "On point!" she gasped. "This case reverses the chief case decided by the appellate division upon which the prosecution is relying!" Sara read the decision, made two photocopies, and tucked them in her briefcase. Such a coincidence had only happened once before, she recalled. In that instance, a case decided by the Court of Appeals a few days earlier provided only supplemental support for her argument where the question was the application in state court of the automatic stay by a bankruptcy court.

People v. Bolden, decided yesterday, was right on target of the issue she would argue later in the morning.

Sara couldn't mask her excitement as she composed the note she would e-mail to Erica. She could picture the expression on her partner's face — relaxing in Atlanta — when she learned of the almost uncanny timing of her motion and the decision in *Bolden*. Sara completed the e-mail message by attaching a file of the high and low of several common and preferred stock issues. Erica had requested the information to make a decision as to whether to use the date-of-death or alternate valuations on an estate tax return.

Sara composed another short message to a lawyer representing a bank. Her clients are purchasing a house and the bank's lawyer needed the real property description by 9 a.m. Sara had received the description from the seller's attorney when she checked her e-mail late yesterday afternoon. She attached it to her comments on a couple of title questions that had been raised.

Sara sent the messages and still had time to complete one more task. She needed information about a few of the components of the consumer price index to calculate a rental adjustment for a client's commercial lease. She had noticed in last night's paper that the Bureau of Labor Statistics had released last month's figures yesterday morning. Sara logged on to the Labor Department's bulletin board system (BBS) — one of several available from federal and state agencies — and downloaded the entire report in less than a minute. As she was copying the report to a diskette, Dick, her legal assistant, arrived at the office.

She handed the diskette to Dick and asked him to pull the relevant numbers from the report and prepare the calculations for the rental adjustment. "Draft a cover letter to the lessee, and I'll review everything after my court appearance on the motion."

When Karen arrived a few minutes later, Sara told her of the *Bolden* case. Karen had assisted her in preparing the memorandum of law on the motion.

"Are you kidding?" Karen asked.

Karen had performed some searches on the legal issue on a CD-ROM and was aware of the decision of the Second Department in *Bolden*. She shared Sara's excitement in learning that the decision had been reversed just yesterday.

"I guess you can eliminate the part of your argument stressing your reasons why *Bolden* shouldn't be followed," Karen remarked. Though *Bolden* wasn't a Fourth Department case, it had seemed to Karen that the county court judge would probably rely on the Second Department holding in *Bolden* because the facts were practically identical to those in Sara's case.

"Now that has changed," Karen mused to herself, realizing that Sara would be relying on the Court of Appeals reversal and that she had been able to get the information before the assistant D.A. would be able to read a brief summary of the case in the *New York Law Journal* or find it on Westlaw or Lexis.

On her way to court, Sara reflected on the implementation of computers in the office since she and Erica first began using them to communicate. Shortly after they began downloading cases decided by the Court of Appeals, they acquired software that would allow them to search the cases. They now have on the hard drive of one computer all cases decided by the Court since June 1990, in fully searchable form.

The search software also allowed them to create other information bases. They now routinely add all briefs and memoranda of law, internal memos resulting from legal research, and selected items of factual research. Previously, they had to rely on memory to locate the products of prior research.

"What was the name of the case we handled a few years ago involving the Martin Act?" was a typical question. After everyone in the office was disrupted from work to jog their collective memories, most often — though not always — someone would recall the client's name. The file would be retrieved from storage and only then could the benefits of prior research be helpful. Now it is only necessary to search for the term "Martin Act" and all occurrences of the phrase in the entire information base are immediately available.

One computer equipped with a CD-ROM drive is dedicated to research. It is a very manageable arrangement with only two lawyers in the firm. Sara and Erica each have computers in their offices equipped with a modem. Karen and Dick use their computers primarily for word processing, accounting and specialized spreadsheets.

"Thank you, your Honor." Sara remarked after Judge Grisham ruled favorably on her motion. The assistant district attorney was still reeling as Sara left the courtroom to return to her office. Sara's client didn't understand exactly what she had done. He did realize that "something happened" that impressed the judge and took the prosecutor by surprise. He would never fully appreciate how his lawyer's use of technology had just prevented him from spending at least a short stint in the county jail.

Sara signed her outgoing mail and glanced at the new rental figures Dick had worked up. "That saved some time," she thought. Three years ago Dick was on the phone for nearly 30 minutes trying to get the correct numbers from the Bureau of Labor Statistics. The computer eliminated all that hassle.

Sara checked her e-mail and had only one message. It was from Erica.

> Sara, CONGRATULATIONS!!! You're doing so well in my absence that you probably want me to stay on vacation an extra week. <grin> Seriously, the Magnificent Seven couldn't have timed it better for you.
>
> Could you do me a favor? Mark and I met another couple from St. Louis. They seem like nice people, though a little showy money-wise. Could you do a paper search in the *St. Louis Post-Dispatch* and let me know what you come up with, if anything? The names are Dean and Deborah Defebo. Thanks.
>
> See you soon,
>
> Erica

Sara printed the message and placed it near her computer as a reminder to run the search later.

Appointments were scheduled for the balance of the afternoon. Sara returned to the office after dinner to put the finishing touches on an appellate brief. She had completed it a few days ago, and had purposely put it aside to finalize with a fresh point of view.

The brief was just that — brief — consisting of only two pages of text. After the first draft had been completed, she sought advice about the length of the brief in the "lawyers only" section of a commercial BBS. Several responses from lawyers around the country assured her that a two-page brief is fine if all points on appeal are covered. The consensus was that the judges of the appellate court would appreciate less reading and more substance.

As she read the comments of other lawyers, Sara mused that her computer allowed her to bounce ideas with scores of other lawyers. "Sort of like an electronic partnership where several lawyers provide a point of view," she thought.

After a few minor changes, Sara put the draft on Dick's desk with a note to send the final version to the printer.

Sara checked the law BBS for new messages and quickly responded to one on a real property question. Then she accessed a different service and entered the information base for the *St. Louis Post-Dispatch.* The service has several hundred information bases in numerous disciplines, many highly specialized, including newspapers published in major metropolitan areas. Access is inexpensive after 6 p.m. local time.

She ran a search for the names Erica provided and got two "hits." After logging off she read them and chuckled at the results. According to a wedding announcement, the couple from St. Louis were married there about two years ago. The other article featured them when they won a million dollars in the Illinois lottery eight months ago! "That explains the 'high-roller' observation that Erica made," Sara sighed. She e-mailed the text of the articles to Erica with a cryptic comment to the effect that Erica might try to nurture the couple as new clients. That done, Sara ended her day at the office.

Later that evening, Erica logged on to a commercial service from her hotel room in Atlanta using her laptop. She was specifically checking the medical bulletin board for any responses to a question she had posed concerning a client diagnosed with bipolar disorder. A psychiatrist had responded that alcohol should be avoided since the client was using lithium and another medication. "In no case should alcohol consumption exceed the equivalent of four units (one unit = one ounce of 80-proof liquor) per week," the psychiatrist cautioned.

After logging off, Erica saved the psychiatrist's message and read the note from Sara and the articles from the *St. Louis Post-Dispatch*. She and Mark shared a laugh as they learned the source of their newly found friends' financial resources.

Sara wrapped up her evening at home editing a bulletin on the latest decisions of the Court of Appeals in the area of criminal law. She started the bulletin as a service to the bench and bar a few years ago by placing them in the county law library. After a while a few lawyers suggested that she might mail or fax the bulletin to the criminal bar as a subscription service. Though not a revenue producer as a publication, it had resulted in referrals of clients from other lawyers.

How to Get Up and Running On-line — A Primer

Terminology

The basic requirements for communicating with a computer entail software and hardware. The software is referred to as "communication software" and the hardware is referred to as a "modem." There are numerous varieties of each on the market and any should be suitable. If you do not already own a modem, it is recommended that you obtain one that is capable of exchanging information at the rate of 9,600 bits per second (bps).

Once installed, you are ready to connect with any computer that is accessible on-line. All that is required is a one-time setup of your communication software to enable your computer to call the host computer and communicate with it. Although this may sound a bit technical, it is not. Again, setting the parameters with your communication software is done once, and you can forget about it after that.

Court of Appeals Computer

Let's go through the steps of connecting to the Court of Appeals. Open your communication software and name the settings you will make — for example, COURTAPP or Court of Appeals, depending on how many spaces the software permits. Next enter the phone number: 1-518-426-2220. If you must dial "8" or "9" to get an outside line, enter the number as 8,,1-518-426-2220. (The commas initiate a pause to allow time to transfer from the inside line to an outside line.) One caution: If you use "call waiting," it should be disabled while you are on-line with any computer. That feature, if activated while on-line, will terminate your connection if another call comes in.

The next setting is "terminal emulation." Select DEC VT-100(ANSI). If that does not appear as one of the choices in your communication software, then use the default choice.

Communications settings are: speed — use 2,400 or 9,600 bps (sometimes referred to as baud rate); data bits — select 8; stop bits — select 1; parity — select none.

Use the default settings of your communication software for all other parameters and save all of the settings. You are now ready to communicate with the computer maintained by the Court of Appeals. It operates continuously. Simply direct your communications software to call the Court of Appeals. This is done by selecting the choice "call," "dial," "phone," or some similar command.

Once connected, you will be asked to supply your first name, then last name, and finally your password. The password may be any combination of numerals and/or letters that you select yourself. You will then view messages placed recently and may proceed to the next screens by pressing the "return" or "enter" key on your computer until you come to the main menu. Selections from the main menu may be made as you please, except you may not download decisions until you subscribe to the service. The fee is $50 per year.

Since 1991, Court of Appeals decisions may be downloaded from a commercial service, GEnie (General Electric Network Information Exchange). They are located in the library of the Law RoundTable.

Search Software

The Court of Appeals computer maintains an inventory of decisions made within the last six months or so. They are not in searchable form; they're simply there for you to download to your computer.

Once you have captured them to the hard drive on your computer, you can create a searchable information base by using commercial software designed for that purpose. "ZyIndex" and "Ask Sam" are examples of such products. In addition to creating a searchable information base of Court of Appeals cases, you may create other information bases such as the "law & fact" base used in Sara's office to search for the case that involved the Martin Act.

Commercial Services

There are a number of commercial services available. This article is based on the author's use of two of them, GEnie and CompuServe. All of the major services offer e-mail to other subscribers as well as through the Internet. Internet e-mail access allows mail to be sent to and received from about 22 million users worldwide.

A word about e-mail to those not familiar with it: Electronic mail is the electronic equivalent of the physical letter or package that might be sent through the U.S. Postal Service. Each user has an electronic mailbox with a distinct address. To send e-mail it is only necessary to know the address of the intended recipient. With service-specific front-end software, the letter can be drafted off-line. After revisions and corrections are made, it is then sent.

Depending on the software, all that is required is depressing one or two keys to send e-mail. The software connects you to the service, logs in your identification and password, sends the e-mail message(s), and automatically logs you off in, typically, 10 to 30 seconds.

Your message is immediately placed in the recipient's electronic mailbox if the recipient subscribes to the same commercial service. If the message goes through the Internet mail system, delivery time usually varies from less than a minute to 15 minutes. Delivery time on the Internet depends on the volume of mail being handled by the system at the time.

Receiving e-mail is just as simple. Depress one or two keys and your computer logs on to the service and retrieves all mail in your mailbox. You may check your mail as frequently as you think necessary. Keep in mind that some services purge mail not collected after a period of time, so an extended absence may cause you to miss mail.

Another e-mail feature is "attaching a file," which is the electronic equivalent of sending a cover letter with an enclosure. The enclosure may be a text document or a binary file. A text file is purely text without enhancements such as underscoring, italics, specialized fonts, etc. Documents created on your word processor are sent as a binary file where all such enhancements will be preserved. The only caution in sending a binary file is that the recipient must also use the same software as that used to create the document — for example, a contract produced with Microsoft Word cannot be used on the recipient's computer using WordPerfect. The solution in such a case is to use the "save as" command to create a text-only document but, again, all enhancements will be lost.

One advantage of using e-mail instead of a fax machine is that the document is received in machine-readable form. There is no need to re-keyboard anything, with the obvious result of saving time and money.

Binary files are any machine-readable files other than text files. Software or software output can be sent as files — any program can be sent, as well as data for a spreadsheet, graphical information, and any information that can be reduced to computer language.

Mention should be made of commercial services dedicated to the profession. Lexis and Westlaw are the two well-known on-line services, but others are developing less comprehensive, though servicable, information bases at usage rates that are much more affordable for the solo practitioner or small firm. LLR OnLine (call 206-462-7714 for information) began a few years ago and now has U.S. Supreme Court and federal circuit court decisions available in searchable form. Also available are decisions from the highest court in several states, including New York. The *New York Law Journal* is on-line with its subscription service, Law Journal EXTRA! (call 212-843-8400 for information). Current and archived editions of *New York Law Journal* and *National Law Journal* are available in searchable form. The service also provides access to legal materials available on the Internet.

The Internet

Said to be the precursor of the so-called "information superhighway," the Internet is a connection that exists among thousands of computers worldwide. The Internet makes these computers available to an estimated 22 million global users. The body of knowledge and factual information available is massive.

In the field of law, the pioneering effort on the Internet has been made by Professor Peter W. Martin of the Legal Information Institute (LII) at Cornell University. Martin and a colleague, Thomas R. Bruce, are developing the equivalent of an electronic law library and teaching resource. Though still in its developmental stage, this information base and directory portend a powerful tool for the solo or small-firm attorney.

The technology is impressive yet transparent to the user. For example, full-text searches of all U.S. Supreme Court cases decided since June 1990, may be performed by accessing the LII computer at Cornell. The cases are actually archived on a computer at Case Western Reserve University. When a search is formulated, the Cornell computer accesses and searches the CWR computer and displays the results — all of this occurring without the user having any idea that the Cornell and CWR computers are working together.

Chapter Seven

The Ethics of Marketing Legal Services

by Russell G. Pearce and Bruce A. Green[1]

THIS CHAPTER OFFERS guidance on the ethics of marketing legal services in terms of both the moral choices and New York regulatory requirements confronting lawyers. The history of professional discourse regarding, and regulation of, lawyer marketing derives from notions that the open marketing of legal services itself is unprofessional and unethical.[2] This background and market considerations make it a matter of self-interest, as well as morality, for lawyers who market to seek the high moral ground. They should use dignified and truthful marketing strategies and provide high-quality services. At the same time, one manifestation of the traditional antipathy to marketing is a highly technical and sometimes confusing regulatory system. With regard to the various forms of marketing, we identify prohibited conduct, "safe harbors," and "slippery slopes," as well as potential constitutional challenges to existing regulations.

The Ethics of Marketing Legal Services

This section discusses the ethics of marketing legal services from the perspective of ethics as moral judgment. We join the United States Supreme Court,[3] the American Bar Association ("ABA"),[4] and other commentators[5] who reject the approach of many in the bar who assert that marketing is in and of itself unethical and unprofessional.[6] Instead, we believe that marketing is an appropriate way for lawyers to provide consumers with information they may need to choose a lawyer.[7]

In general, we suggest three rules for ethical marketing. Adherence to these rules serves your professional self-interest, fulfills your moral obligations, and limits your exposure to professional discipline and malpractice liability.[8]

One: Marketing efforts should be truthful and should not have even an appearance of being misleading.[9] The prudent lawyer will go beyond the minimal standard set forth in the Code of Professional Responsibility for avoiding false and misleading communications and ensure that all communications are as comprehensible and fair as possible. A lawyer should therefore avoid communications that are to any reasonable degree potentially misleading.

Two: Marketing strategies should not undermine the dignity of the individual lawyer or the legal profession.[10] Undignified advertising undermines the respect that you should have for yourself as a lawyer, as well as the respect of the profession and the public.

Three: Consumers recruited through marketing should receive high-quality services.[11] Lawyers who market need to anticipate the demand for their services resulting from marketing and prepare to provide high-quality services to those who seek them.

While the morality of these rules is self-evident, they also serve the lawyer's self-interest.

First, in the market for legal services, truthful and dignified advertising that results in high-quality services will be the most profitable. Undignified marketing for the practitioner and the profession may serve to lower the opinion of lawyers among members of the public.[12] Similarly, questionable claims and lack of high-quality services are likely to prove counterproductive. Marketing claims are likely to increase client expectations, and if the expectations are not satisfied, the client will be disappointed. Furthermore, marketing magnifies the impact of client dissatisfaction, whether from misleading claims or from inadequate services. Studies of consumer responses to advertising show a relationship between advertising and word-of-mouth reputation: The increased exposure generated by advertising helps word-of-mouth reputation (good or bad) spread faster.[13] Marketing thus could have the ironic consequence of *decreasing* business for a less than candid marketer or poor performer.[14]

Second, marketing that does not meet the standards we suggest may expose the lawyer to increased risk of professional discipline and malpractice liability. As noted above, significant anti-marketing sentiment exists within the profession, and therefore one might expect that many lawyers will be more likely to take a hard look at the conduct of lawyers who market and to file complaints with disciplinary authorities about such lawyers.[15] In addition, the failure of a lawyer to provide the services promised might encourage the client to complain to disciplinary authorities or to sue for malpractice.

Accordingly, high ethical standards in marketing are both the moral and the profitable strategy.

Sources of Authority

The United States Constitution

Throughout most of this century, states prohibited attorney advertising.[16] This prohibition derived largely from the perception of bar leaders that advertising was inherently unethical.[17] In 1977, in *Bates v. State Bar of Arizona*,[18] the United States Supreme Court rejected this view, holding that the First Amendment to the United States Constitution protects lawyer marketing as commercial speech, and overturned state bans on lawyer advertising.[19]

The basis for commercial speech protection is that a "free flow of commercial information"[20] serves the public interest. A state may restrict or prohibit false, deceptive, or misleading commercial speech because such speech contributes nothing of value to the public.[21] The Constitution, however, limits the degree to which a state may restrict "[c]ommercial speech that is not false, deceptive, or misleading."[22] The state has the burden of demonstrating that any such restriction "directly and materially advances a substantial state interest in a manner no more extensive than necessary to serve that interest."[23] To meet this burden, "the State 'must demonstrate that the harms it recites are real and that its restriction will in fact alleviate them to a material degree.'"[24]

Applying this test, or earlier, similar versions of it, the Supreme Court has invalidated various restrictions on the marketing of legal services, including prohibitions on the advertising of the price and availability of services[25] and the use of targeted direct mail.[26] The Court has, however, upheld a ban on in-person solicitation of cases for profit,[27] while overturning restrictions on solicitation for *pro bono* efforts as protected political expression.[28]

The Supreme Court's analysis *may* be in the process of becoming more tolerant of state restrictions on lawyer marketing. In the recent case of *Florida Bar v. Went for It, Inc.*,[29] the United States Supreme Court upheld Florida rules "creat[ing] a 30-day blackout period after an accident during which lawyers may not, directly or indirectly, single out accident victims or their relatives in order to solicit their business."[30] In upholding the rules, the Court employed the same test it had previously used in lawyer marketing cases. With regard to the first prong of the test, that "the government must assert a substantial interest in support of the regulation,"[31] the Court found "substantial" Florida's "interest in protecting the privacy and tranquility of personal injury victims and their loved ones against intrusive, unsolicited contact by lawyers"[32] and in protecting the bar's reputation from the demeaning effect of "direct mail solicitations in the wake of accidents."[33]

The Court further found that the Florida restrictions satisfied the second prong of the test requiring that "the government must demonstrate that the restriction on commercial speech directly and materially advances that interest."[34] As evidence that "'the harms . . . are real and that [the] restriction[s] will in fact alleviate them to a material degree,'"[35] the Court relied on a Florida survey finding negative attitudes toward direct mail advertising, as well as an extensive anecdotal record, including editorials critical of direct mail solicitation of accident victims and individual complaints regarding such marketing.

Last, the Court found that the restrictions satisfied the third prong of the test requiring that the restrictions "be 'narrowly drawn.'"[36] The Court observed that "[t]he Bar's rule is reasonably well tailored to its stated objective of eliminating targeted mailings whose type and timing are a source of distress to Floridians, distress that has caused many of them to lose respect for the legal profession."[37]

Accordingly, one could read the *Florida Bar* decision narrowly as a continuation of existing doctrine. It applies the same test the Court had previously used and does not overrule prior precedents. Rather, in light of both the particular regulation and the extensive evidence supporting it, the Court for the first time in recent years upheld a restriction on lawyer advertising.

However, one could also read the opinion as the harbinger of a newer, more restrictive approach to lawyer advertising. In dissent, Justice Kennedy described the decision as "a major retreat from the constitutional guarantees for commercial speech[.]"[38] Describing the Florida Bar's approach as self-serving censorship, Justice Kennedy rejected the Court's finding of a substantial interest in the Florida restrictions on direct mail solicitation and described the Florida Bar evidence as "noteworthy for its incompetence."[39] Justice Kennedy observed that "[t]here is no authority for the proposition that the Constitution permits the State to promote the public image of the legal profession by suppressing information about the profession's business aspects."[40]

As the dissent suggests, the *Florida Bar* opinion could represent the beginning of a major shift in the Court's jurisprudence. The Court for the first time accorded significant weight to the public perception of the profession as a legitimate ground for restricting lawyer marketing.[41] This argument could be used to challenge or restrict other forms of marketing, including advertising. Indeed, Justice O'Connor, who wrote the *Florida Bar* opinion, as well as Chief Justice Rehnquist and Justice Scalia, who were also in the majority, have previously called for the

Court to reconsider its initial decision to strike down barriers to lawyer advertising.[42]

New York Authority

A lawyer's marketing efforts are subject to the New York Lawyer's Code of Professional Responsibility[43] (hereinafter "Code"), Canon 2, and the Disciplinary Rules of Canon 2 (hereinafter "DR"), as well as section 479 of the Judiciary Law.[44] In addition, state and local bar association ethics committees have issued opinions applying the Code to particular situations in light of federal constitutional considerations. These opinions do not have the force of law, but they are often persuasive to courts and disciplinary authorities. Disciplinary authorities are generally reluctant to impose sanctions on lawyers who follow advice from ethics committees that the disciplinary authorities later find to be erroneous.

Finally, a lawyer who advertises is subject to the requirements of certain consumer protection statutes.[45]

Marketing Techniques

Any communication to a non-lawyer for the purpose of obtaining business implicates the ethical rules governing marketing. This part will discuss prohibited and permissible marketing techniques. Telephone or in-person solicitation of business is generally prohibited. Advertising, brochures, direct-mail marketing, public speaking, seminars, articles, signs, and business cards are generally acceptable under limitations described below. The section entitled "Marketing Content" (below) will discuss regulation of the content of these marketing strategies.

Personal Communication to Individuals

Prohibited Conduct

With limited exceptions discussed below, a lawyer may not ask a potential client for business in person or by telephone, nor may an agent do so on the lawyer's behalf. In *Ohralik v. Ohio State Bar Association*,[46] the United States Supreme Court upheld a ban on in-person solicitation by lawyers.[47] The lawyer in *Ohralik* was a personal injury practitioner who solicited the business of a young woman who was in the hospital recovering from an accident (which was to be the subject of the lawyer's employment).[48] The basis for this decision was the importance of protecting the vulnerable accident victim from overreaching and fraud.[49]

Unfortunately, the New York provisions on solicitation are a bit confusing. The lawyer must look to several Code provisions and a statutory section: DR 2-103(A), DR 2-103(C), DR 2-104(A), and section 479 of the Judiciary Law.[50] The relevant Code sections do little more than make statutory or court rule violations into disciplinary violations. DR 2-103(A) provides that "[a] lawyer shall not, directly or indirectly, seek professional employment for the lawyer or a partner or associate of the lawyer from a person who has not sought advice regarding employment of the lawyer" if such efforts are contrary to statute or court rule.[51] DR 2-104(A) similarly provides that "[a] lawyer who has given unsolicited advice to an individual to obtain counsel or take legal action shall not accept employment resulting from that advice" if such effort is contrary to statute or court rule.[52] The statute that prohibits solicitation and therefore makes it impermissible under these sections is section 479 of the Judiciary Law, which broadly prohibits solicitation by or on behalf of a lawyer.[53] In addition, DR 2-103(C) prohibits a lawyer from asking others to promote the lawyer's services "other than by advertising or [public communications]."[54] These provisions prohibit in-person or telephone marketing of services to an individual. These provisions also prohibit asking third parties in writing to solicit legal business.[55]

Violations of the prohibition on solicitation have resulted in a significant number of disciplinary prosecutions.[56]

Safe Harbors

A limited number of exceptions to the ban on solicitation offer attorneys narrow safe harbors. Probably the most useful is the exception for solicitation of business from a "former client (if the advice is germane to the former employment)," as well as from "a close friend [or] relative."[57] Also permissible is solicitation of clients for "litigation in the nature of a class action . . . if success in asserting rights or defenses of a client . . . is dependent upon the joinder of others."[58]

A lawyer may also solicit business from approved lawyer referral services,[59] other lawyers, and legal services organizations.[60] Similarly, an open panel prepaid plan[61] or a lawyer referral service[62] may solicit on a lawyer's behalf.

Despite language in the New York Code suggesting limitations on solicitation for *pro bono* purposes,[63] the United States Supreme Court has found such limitations unacceptable.[64]

Trends and Constitutional Challenges

A recent Supreme Court decision striking down a ban on solicitation by accountants[65] suggests that the Court might be willing to limit *Ohralik* to solicitation of individuals, as opposed to businesses, or even to solicitation of vulnerable individuals.[66] Commentators have similarly suggested that the rationale of protecting vulnerable clients does not apply to solicitation of business clients.[67]

On the other hand, the decision in *Florida Bar v. Went for It, Inc.*[68] may indicate that the Court is now more willing to uphold restrictions on lawyer marketing than it has been in the past.

Communications to Groups and Written Communications to Individuals

As a general rule, communications to groups and written communications to individuals are permissible. This part will discuss technical regulations of these marketing techniques. Content restrictions are discussed in "Marketing Content," *infra*.

Print and Broadcast Advertising

The New York Code generally permits print and broadcast advertising.[69]

1. *Technical Regulations.* All broadcast advertising must be "prerecorded or taped and approved for broadcast by the lawyer."[70] The lawyer must retain "a recording or videotape of the actual transmission [of broadcast advertising] for a period of not less than one year following such transmission."[71]
2. *Slippery Slope: Group Advertising.* A number of attorneys appear to be using group advertising, in which individual lawyers or law firms join together to pay for a single advertisement. Generally, the advertisement promotes a single telephone number from which the consumer will be referred to a specific lawyer or law firm. The problem with this advertising is that it appears to function like a private referral service, and the New York Code bars private lawyer referral services that have not been approved by the bar.[72] Balancing the ban on private referral services with the need of small firms to pool resources to afford advertising, the New York State Bar Ethics Committee has suggested it would approve a group advertisement that

   > presents in a meaningful fashion the names of the lawyers or law firms participating in the group advertisement, along with their addresses and the geographical areas assigned to them, so that the potential client knows the identity of the lawyer to whom his call will be referred and there is no discretion in referrals on the part of the advertising agents.[73]

   Ethics committees have found inadequate group advertising proposals that have not met this standard.[74]

Direct Mail

The Supreme Court has held that while states may not generally prohibit lawyers from targeting direct mail to specific consumers,[75] they may impose reasonable restrictions on such marketing, such as prohibiting contact with accident victims within 30 days of their accident.[76] The New York Code, however, generally permits the use of direct mail marketing.[77]

Technical Regulations. At the time of initial distribution, lawyers must file with the appropriate Departmental Disciplinary Committee copies of mailings, leaflets, brochures and any other advertising that is not published in periodicals or broadcast.[78] They must also retain on file for at least one year any address list used for distributing these materials.[79]

Leaflets and Brochures

1. *Technical Regulations.* The New York Code generally permits the use of leaflets and brochures subject to the regulations discussed under "Direct Mail," above.
2. *Safe Harbor and Slippery Slope: Use of third parties to distribute materials.* An attorney may use third parties to distribute brochures and fliers. These parties, however, may not discuss the brochures and fliers.[80] If they are receiving compensation for distributing the brochures and fliers, "it must be clear from the circumstances that the third party is neither endorsing nor recommending the use of the lawyer's services."[81]

Professional Notices, Business Cards, Signs, and Letterhead

Subject to content-based restrictions, lawyers generally may display signs in or near their offices,[82] use cards to make announcements about their practice,[83] and distribute business cards to potential clients.[84] Ethics authorities approve the use of signs at public events as a form of advertising, provided that the signs are not false or misleading.[85]

Public Speaking, Seminars, and Publications

A lawyer generally may speak to groups or publish articles and then accept resulting employment.[86] These activities must be "designed to educate the public to recognize legal problems, to make intelligent selection of counsel or to utilize available legal services."[87] The rules that permit these activities appear to permit lawyers to provide seminars for free or for a fee either to potential clients or to other professionals.[88]

Prohibited Conduct. In public speaking or publications, a lawyer may not give individual advice.[89]

900 Numbers

The New York State Bar Ethics Committee has opined that "[a] lawyer may record a message to be played on a 900 telephone number which provides general information about a particular area of law."[90] In doing so, the "lawyer should be careful not to appear to offer individual advice."[91] If the message includes an advertisement for the lawyer, it is subject to the regulations for advertisements.[92] The Ethics Committee further opined that "[a] lawyer may accept a fee from the owner of a 900 number for preparing a recorded message [or] share in profits generated by calls to the number."[93]

Auction of Services

Prohibited Conduct. A lawyer may not auction his or her services, even on behalf of a charity.[94]

MARKETING CONTENT

The general rule is that a lawyer's marketing communications may not be false, deceptive, or misleading.[95] Also, marketing communications "shall include the name, office address and telephone number of the attorney or law firm whose services are being offered."[96]

In marketing legal services, the lawyer wants to distinguish himself or herself from other attorneys so as to persuade the consumer to choose to retain his or her services. A lawyer may seek to achieve this goal in several ways. First, the lawyer may convey facts about his or her practice that indicate a fit with the client's needs, such as office location, office hours, concentration in a field of law, or affordable fees. These claims are generally acceptable. Second, the lawyer may distinguish the firm through its image or quality of services in a way that would make the firm attractive. These types of claims are more problematic, but permissible to a limited degree.

Factual Claims

Prohibited Conduct

False, deceptive, or misleading claims are all prohibited.[97] It is important to remember that a representation, although factually true, may be considered to be misleading.[98] For example, the United States Supreme Court has approved sanctions on a lawyer for claiming that " 'if there is no recovery, no legal fees are owed by our clients.' "[99] The Court reasoned that laypersons unaware "of the distinction between 'legal fees' and 'costs' " would be misled into believing that they would have no financial obligation if they did not recover.[100] New York authorities have similarly disapproved of a lawyer claiming in the Yellow Pages to practice in areas of law where he had no experience[101] and of lawyers using titles for non-lawyers that could potentially mislead the public into believing that they are lawyers.[102]

Safe Harbors

Under the Code and Supreme Court decisions, a lawyer may otherwise safely provide:

1. Educational background, foreign language fluency, organizational affiliations, public offices, and teaching positions.[103] Retired judges may list former judicial positions on their letterheads, provided such listing clearly indicates that the judge is retired and the description of the former judicial title is not misleading.[104] However, when a former judge advertised that he was a former judge, lawyers complained to disciplinary officials, who contacted him regarding his advertisement.[105] As far as we are aware, there has been no public resolution of this matter.
2. Dates of bar admissions.[106] In firms formed or continued between lawyers licensed in different jurisdictions, all listings of partners and associates must clearly state any jurisdictional limitations on any of the lawyers.[107]
3. "[T]he names of clients regularly represented, provided that the client has given prior written consent."[108]
4. Bank references and credit arrangements accepted.[109]
5. Participation in a prepaid or group legal services program.[110]
6. Information about fees,[111] including fees for initial consultation, contingent fee rates ("when accompanied by a statement disclosing whether percentages are computed before or after deduction of costs and disbursements"), range of fees for services ("provided there be available to the public free of charge a written statement clearly describing the scope of each advertised service"), hourly rates, and fixed fees for specified services.[112]
7. Areas of practice. Attorneys may state that they "concentrate in" an area of practice or that their practice is "limited to" a certain area.[113] An attorney may not, however, claim to "specialize" in a certain area.[114]
8. A description of the services the lawyer seeks to provide and the potential benefits to the consumer.[115]
9. In letterheads,[116] an identification of a lawyer as "of counsel" if he or she has a continuing relationship with a lawyer or law firm other than as associate or partner."[117]

10. In client letterheads, a description of a lawyer or law firm as "General Counsel" if the lawyer or firm devotes a substantial amount of professional time to the representation of that client.[118]

Self-Promotion, Image and Quality Claims

General Quality Claims

1. *Prohibited Conduct.* The New York Code prohibits "puffery, self-laudation, claims regarding the quality of the [lawyer's] legal services, and claims that cannot be measured or verified."[119] The New York Code also prohibits lawyer communications that "cast reflection on the bar as a whole."[120] These provisions are quite vague.
2. *Slippery Slopes.* Quality claims are common in advertisements generally. Indeed, we have seen such claims in advertisements by lawyers even though they would violate the letter of the New York Code. The United States Constitution requires that in prosecuting violators of the Code, disciplinary authorities must prove that the claims are false, deceptive, or misleading,[121] or that restrictions on the claims "directly and materially advance[ ] a substantial state interest in a manner no more extensive than necessary to serve that interest."[122] In a recent case, the United States District Court for the Northern District of New York found that disciplinary authorities failed to meet this burden in a proceeding against a lawyer who claimed: "He's a smart, tough lawyer who's on your side," "He's in your corner," and "If you've been injured you deserve a fast, fair compensation[.]"[123]

Testimonials

One particular type of quality claim is a testimonial to the lawyer's success in previous cases. The New York State Bar Ethics Committee has described "testimonials" as "testimonials, endorsements and recommendations which in some manner describe results obtained by the lawyer or assess the lawyer's performance."[124]

1. *Prohibited Conduct.* The New York State Bar Ethics Committee has opined that "a dramatization using a fictional client testimonial [as opposed to a fictional portrayal of an actual client testimonial] is unethical because it is inherently false, deceptive and misleading."[125]
2. *Safe Harbors.*
    - Client testimonials are permissible unless they are "potentially misleading."[126] The New York State Bar Association has offered the following as types of statements that would make a testimonial potentially misleading: "statements of 'overblown assurances of client satisfaction,' statements that create unjustified expectations

or 'false hopes,' or statements that fail to contain sufficient information[.]"[127] Client testimonials should also include a disclaimer to the effect that "facts and prior results in an earlier case do not guarantee or predict a similar outcome with respect to any future matter on which the lawyer may be retained."[128]

- Fictional portrayals of client testimonials are permissible with the client's consent,[129] under the conditions set forth above for client testimonials, and with a clear "caption, announcement[ ], or other disclosure . . . that the presentation is a dramatization of actual events in which the real clients are portrayed by actors."[130]

Illustrations, Photographs, and Fictional Dramatizations

The United States Supreme Court has invalidated prohibitions on the use of illustrations that are not false, deceptive, and misleading.[131] Similarly, the New York State Bar Association Ethics Committee has opined that "[d]ramatizations of fictional events can be used in a radio or television advertisement in much the same way as a drawing or photograph can be used in a print medium to illustrate a situation to the viewer, provided the dramatization is done in a manner that is not false or misleading."[132]

Specialization Claims

1. *Prohibited Conduct.* A lawyer may "hold himself or herself out as a specialist" or use the term "specialize" only if certified "by the authority having jurisdiction under the laws of this state" and "in accordance with the rules prescribed by that authority."[133] We are not aware of any such certification program in New York.
2. *Safe Harbor.* A lawyer can accomplish much the same marketing goal of suggesting a specialty by using the terms "concentrating in" or "limited to" to describe areas of practice.[134]
3. *Slippery Slope.* The Professional Responsibility Committee of The Association of the Bar of the City of New York has observed that despite the language of the New York Code, under a recent Supreme Court decision, "lawyers are now free to advertise verifiable, truthful and noninherently misleading statements concerning private certification [as a specialist]." [135]

Firm and Trade Names

1. *Prohibited Conduct.* As a general rule, lawyers may not use trade names.[136]

2. *Safe Harbors.*
   - Firm names may include the names of deceased or retired partners.[137]
   - The phrase "legal clinic" may be part of a firm name provided the name identifies the lawyer or firm.[138]
3. *Slippery Slopes.* The Court of Appeals permitted a lawyer to use the descriptive phrase "The Country Lawyer" with his firm name on the ground that it would not deceive the public about the identity, responsibility, and status of the lawyer.[139] The Court distinguished this phrase from the impermissible "'The People's Law Firm of Jan L. Shepard, Attorney, P.C.'" on the ground that the phrase "People's Law Firm . . . suggested that the firm was controlled by the public, received public funding or provided legal services on a nonprofit basis."[140] While this decision suggests that non-deceptive descriptive phrases are acceptable, the disciplinary authorities in the Third Department have prosecuted an attorney for using the rather innocuous phrase "A Law Firm" to improve his alphabetical listing in the Yellow Pages.[141]

Potential Liability

The major source of liability for violating the rules discussed above is disciplinary sanction, such as censure, suspension, and disbarment. The safest course is to seek guidance from a bar ethics committee or court if you wish to employ marketing techniques or communications that go beyond the safe harbors.

A lawyer who advertises may also face fines under a variety of consumer protection statutes that prohibit deceptive business practices. These include General Business Law sections 349 and 350 and, in New York City, New York City Administrative Code sections 20-700 to 20-703, enforced by the New York City Department of Consumer Affairs. For example, a New York City lawyer was fined more than $200,000 for continuing to permit publication of an advertisement that included the false and misleading statement that a divorce could be obtained within ten days.[142]

A lawyer who makes quality claims might also be liable to clients or potential clients for breach of warranty based on marketing representations.[143]

Last, of course, is the discipline of the market. Lawyers who market are more likely to lose business if the quality of their services is low.[144] Rather than thriving on repeat and referral business, they will find that their bad reputations spread faster than if they had not marketed their services.[145]

Conclusion

In this chapter, we have provided an overview of the law and ethics of marketing legal services in New York. As the chapter demonstrates, marketing legal services is an area where lawyers can do well by doing good. Attention to the moral and regulatory aspects of marketing legal services will both benefit the lawyer's practice and minimize exposure to liability and business losses.

Endnotes

1. Bruce Green is an Associate Professor of Law, Fordham University School of Law, and Director, Stein Center for Ethics and Public Interest Law. Russell G. Pearce is an Associate Professor of Law, Fordham University School of Law, and Associate Director, Stein Center for Ethics and Public Interest Law. The authors gratefully acknowledge the outstanding contribution of research assistant Nina Keilin, Fordham University School of Law, Class of 1995.

2. *See, e.g.*, Michael J. Powell, *From Patrician to Professional Elite: The Transformation of the New York City Bar Association* 156 (1988) (discussing the view that marketing "manifest[s] a spirit of commercialism foreign to the quiet dignity of the profession").

3. *See Bates v. State Bar of Arizona*, 433 U.S. 350, 371-72 (1977) ("It appears that the ban on advertising originated as a rule of etiquette and not as a rule of ethics. . . . Since the belief that lawyers are somehow 'above' trade has become an anachronism, the historical foundation for the advertising restraint has crumbled.").

4. *See* ABA Model Rules of Professional Conduct Rule 7.2 cmt. (1992) ("To assist the public in obtaining legal services, lawyers should be allowed to make known their services not only through reputation but also through organized information campaigns in the form of advertising. Advertising involves an active quest for clients, contrary to the tradition that a lawyer should not seek clientele. However, the public's need to know about legal services can be fulfilled in part through advertising. This need is particularly acute in the case of persons of moderate means who have not made extensive use of legal services. The interest in expanding public information about legal services ought to prevail over considerations of tradition."). *See also* ABA Aspirational Goals on Advertising (1988) (hereinafter "ABA Goals").

5. *See, e.g.,* Whitney Thier, Comment, *In a Dignified Manner: The Bar, the Court and Lawyer Advertising,* 66 Tulane L. Rev. 527, 540 (1991) ("[A]dvertising, which is considered to be inherently competitive, is considered to be the antithesis of professionalism. . . . Many modern legal scholars have argued that these traditional notions of professionalism are elitist, antiquated, and hypocritical.").

6. *See, e.g.,* Powell, note 2, *supra*, p. 156; Warren E. Burger, *The State of Justice,* A.B.A.J., Mar. 1984, pp. 62, 63 (seeking return to prohibitions on advertising); Harry L. Carrico, *The New Professionalism,* N.Y.S.B.J., Jan. 1990, p. 11 (urging lawyers not to market their services openly); W. Ward Reynoldson, *The Case Against Lawyer Advertising*, A.B.A.J., Jan. 1989, p. 60 (arguing that advertising has sullied the profession). Interestingly, in the nineteenth century, John Marshall provided a testimonial in an advertisement while he was sitting as Chief Justice, and Abraham Lincoln advertised for business. *See* Geoffrey C. Hazard, Jr., Russell G. Pearce, and Jeffrey W. Stempel, *Why Lawyers Should Be Allowed to Advertise: A Market Analysis of Legal Services*, 58 N.Y.U. L. Rev. 1084, 1085 n.2 (1983) (hereinafter "Hazard, et al.").

7. *See* Linda Morton, *Finding a Suitable Lawyer: Why Consumers Can't Always Get What They Want and What the Legal Profession Should Do About It*, 25 U.C. Davis L. Rev. 283, 287-89 (1992) ("Sources such as advertising, attorney directories, referral services and lists of attorneys sanctioned for misconduct could provide . . . information regarding integrity and quality.").

8. Similarly, a number of commentators on business ethics observe that moral business choices are, in the long run, in the self-interest of the business. *See, e.g.*, David Braybrooke, "Ethics in the World of Business" 74-75 (1983); Robert Almeder, "Morality in the Marketplace," in *Business Ethics: Corporate Values and Society,* 91-92, Milton Snoeyenbos, et al., eds. (1983).

9. *See* ABA Goals, note 4, *supra.*

10. *See id.*

11. This advice exceeds the standard advocated by the ABA Goals, which suggest only that "[l]awyers should design their advertising to attract legal matters which they are competent to handle." *Id.* We find high quality a more appropriate moral and self-interested aspiration.

12. *See, e.g.*, Gary A. Hengstler, *The Public Perception of Lawyers: ABA Poll*, A.B.A.J., Sept. 1993, pp. 60, 63 (discussing public dissatisfaction with lawyers and lawyer advertising).

13. *See* Hazard et al., *supra* note 6, p. 1099. Van O'Steen, who was one of the petitioners in *Bates v. State Bar of Arizona*, 433 U.S. 350 (1977), the seminal Supreme Court case on lawyer advertising, points out that satisfied clients are the lawyer's best source of referrals. *See* James Podgers, *Image Problem*, A.B.A.J., Feb. 1994, pp. 66, 70.

14. *See* Hazard et al., note 6, *supra* p. 1099.

15. *See* Harry J. Haynsworth, *Marketing and Legal Ethics: The Rules and Risks* 46-47 (1990).

16. *See* Hazard et al., pp. 1084-85.

17. *See Bates v. State Bar of Arizona*, 433 U.S. 350, 367-81 (1977) (discussion of traditional objections to advertising: adverse effect on professionalism, that it was inherently misleading, that it would stir up litigation, and that it would have undesirable economic effects). *But see* note 6 above for discussion of leading nineteenth-century lawyers who participated in advertising legal services.

18. 433 U.S. 350 (1977).

19. *See id.* pp. 384-85.

20. *Zauderer v. Office of Disciplinary Counsel of Supreme Court*, 471 U.S. 626, 646 (1985).

21. *See Friedman v. Rogers*, 440 U.S. 1, 9 (1979) (citing *Gertz v. Robert Welch, Inc.*, 418 U.S. 323, 340 (1974) and *Konigsberg v. State Bar*, 366 U.S. 36, 49 & n.10 (1961) ("Untruthful speech, commercial or otherwise, has never been protected for its own sake.")).

22. *Ibanez v. Florida Dep't of Business & Professional Regulation*, 114 S. Ct. 2084, 2088 (1994).

23. *Id.*

24. *Id.* pp. 2088-89 (quoting *Edenfield v. Fane*, 113 S. Ct. 1792, 1798 (1993)).

25. *See Bates v. State Bar of Arizona*, 433 U.S. 350, 384 (1977).

26. *See Shapero v. Kentucky Bar Ass'n*, 486 U.S. 466, 476 (1988). In this chapter we identify only some of the New York regulations that

are subject to constitutional challenge. However, any rule that goes beyond prohibition of false, deceptive, and misleading marketing conceivably invites constitutional scrutiny.

27. *See Ohralik v. Ohio State Bar Ass'n*, 436 U.S. 447, 449 (1978).

28. *See In re Primus*, 436 U.S. 412, 439 (1978).

29. 115 S. Ct. 2371 (1995).

30. *Id.* at 2374.

31. *Id.* at 2376.

32. *Id.*

33. *Id.*

34. *Id.*

35. *Id.* at 2377 (citing *Rubin v. Coors Brewing Co.*, 115 S. Ct. 1585, 1592) (1995)).

36. *Id.* at 2376.

37. *Id.* at 2380.

38. *Id.* at 2386.

39. *Id.* at 2384.

40. *Id.* at 2386.

41. *Id.*

42. *See Shapero v. Kentucky Bar Ass'n,* 486 U.S. 466, 487 (1988) (O'Connor, J., dissenting).

43. The Lawyer's Code of Professional Responsibility, DR 2-101, DR 2-102, DR 2-103, DR 2-104, and DR 2-105 (1993). The Code has been promulgated as joint rules of the Appellate Division of the New York Supreme Court and set forth in N.Y. Comp. Codes R. & Regs. part 1200, title 22. Hereafter when citing to the Code of Professional Responsibility, this chapter will refer specifically to DRs or generally to the "New York Code" or the "Code." This chapter does not analyze practice under the ABA Model Rules of Professional Conduct, which most states have adopted. The Rules impose a simpler regulatory approach than that found in Code states like New York. For a discussion of the applicable Rules, *see* Geoffrey C. Hazard, Jr., and W. William Hodes, *The Law of Lawyering: A Handbook on the Model Rules of Professional Conduct* Part 7 (2d ed. 1990 and Supp. 1994).

44. *See* Judiciary Law § 479.

45. *See* notes 142-43, *infra,* and accompanying text.

46. 436 U.S. 447 (1978).

47. *See id.* at 455.

48. *See id.* at 449-50.

49. *See id.* at 464-66.

50. Another potential area of confusion is the broad language of these provisions. On their face, DR 2-103(A) and DR 2-104(A) appear to prohibit not only in-person and telephone solicitation, but also marketing techniques, such as print and broadcast advertising, that are constitutionally protected. DR 2-103, however, includes a saving clause stating that it should not be construed to prohibit advertising. *See* DR 2-103(F). On its face, Judiciary Law § 479 prohibits not only solicitation, but also constitutionally protected marketing, such as advertising.

51. DR 2-103(A).

52. DR 2-104(A).

53. Judiciary Law § 479. *See* note 50 above for discussion of the reach of § 479.

54. DR 2-103(C).

55. *See In re Greene*, 54 N.Y.2d 118, 444 N.Y.S.2d 883, 429 N.E.2d 390 (1981) (disciplining attorney who wrote to real estate brokers asking for referrals).

56. *See, e.g., In re Rapport*, 186 A.D.2d 344, 588 N.Y.S.2d 436 (3d Dep't 1992) (ordering censure of attorneys who employed an agent to solicit clients for personal injury cases involving L-tryptophan poisoning); *In re Von Wiegen*, 146 A.D.2d 901, 537 N.Y.S.2d 76 (3d Dep't 1989) (ordering five-year suspension of attorney who employed agent to solicit accident victims for personal injury cases); *In re Kronenberg*, 136 A.D.2d 264, 527 N.Y.S.2d 44 (2d Dep't 1988) (ordering one-year suspension of attorney who hired a civilian employee of the New York City Police Department to refer cases); *In re Kressner*, 108 A.D.2d 334, 111 A.D.2d 730, 489 N.Y.S.2d 194 (1st Dep't 1985) (ordering three-year suspension of an attorney who solicited personal injury victims for medical malpractice claims); *In re Mandell*, 103 A.D.2d 193, 479 N.Y.S.2d 69 (2d Dep't 1984), *appeal dismissed*, 64 N.Y.2d 815, 486 N.Y.S.2d

938, 476 N.E.2d 337 (1985) (ordering three-year suspension of lawyer who solicited employee of a charitable organization to funnel potential clients from among those allegedly injured by other employees of the organization).

57. DR 2-104(B); *see also* New York County Lawyers' Ass'n Comm. on Professional Ethics, Op. 679 (1990) (attorney may solicit business from clients of attorney's former firm; opinion does not offer advice as to whether this constitutes tortious interference with contractual rights of former firm). The Court of Appeals has invalidated provisions of partnership contracts generally penalizing former partners from competing with their former firms for the business of that firm's clients. *See Denburg v. Parker Chapin Flattau & Klimpl*, 82 N.Y.2d 375, 604 N.Y.S.2d 900, 624 N.E.2d 995 (1993); *Cohen v. Lord, Day & Lord*, 75 N.Y.2d 95, 551 N.Y.S.2d 157, 550 N.E.2d 410 (1989).

58. DR 2-104(F). This provision requires compliance with DR 2-103(A).

59. DR 2-103(C)(1).

60. DR 2-103(C).

61. DR 2-103(D)(4).

62. DR 2-103(D)(3).

63. The New York Code limits solicitation for *pro bono* efforts to organized groups or recommendation from other lawyers. *See* DR 2-103(C) and (D).

64. *See In re Primus*, 436 U.S. 412, 422-26 (1978).

65. *See Edenfield v. Fane*, 113 S. Ct. 1792, 1802-03 (1993).

66. *See id.*

67. *See, e.g.,* Podgers, note 13, *supra,* pp. 70, 72; Joel M. Gora, *Symposium: The Supreme Court and Local Government Law; the 1992-93 Term, Back from the Brink: Part II*, 10 Touro L. Rev. 459, 472 (1994).

68. 115 S. Ct. 2371 (1995).

69. *See* DR 2-101.

70. DR 2-101(F).

71. *Id.*

72. A lawyer referral service provides consumers with the names of lawyers who offer the service that the caller seeks. Under most existing arrangements, the lawyer then provides an initial consultation for no fee or a low fee. *See* Ad Hoc Comm. on Private Referral Services, *Regulation of Private Legal Referral Services—A Recommendation*, 44 Rec. Ass'n B. City N.Y. 3, 3 (1989). The Code permits lawyer referral services provided that they are operated, sponsored, or approved by a bar association. *See* DR 2-103(C)(1). Ironically, the Code does not require that these bar-approved or bar-sponsored services screen lawyers for quality. *See* Ad Hoc Committee, *supra*, at 18-19 (suggesting such a requirement); NYSBA Comm. on Professional Ethics, Op. 651 (1993) (hereinafter "NYSBA Op.") (noting that no bar association has developed a standard for approving private or for-profit services). In 1993, the American Bar Association adopted Model Rules Governing Lawyer Referral and Information Services to serve as the basis of state legislation. The Model Rules would require qualified legal referral services to establish qualification standards. As of yet, New York State has not adopted such a requirement, although legal referral services such as the Legal Referral Service, operated jointly by The Association of the Bar of the City of New York and the New York County Lawyers' Association, have adopted such standards.

73. NYSBA Op. 597 (1989).

74. *See* Ass'n B. City N.Y. Comm. on Professional and Judicial Ethics, Formal Op. 1994-3 (1994); Nassau County B.A. Comm. on Professional Ethics, Ops. 93-44 (1994), 93-32 (1993); *see also* Nassau County B.A. Op. 84-1 (1984) (disapproving a divorce resource center that would include lawyer referrals and other services by non-lawyers).

75. *Shapero v. Kentucky Bar Ass'n,* 486 U.S. 466, 467-74 (1988) (holding that a state could not prohibit a lawyer from writing to defendants in foreclosure suits offering his services).

76. *Florida Bar v. Went for It, Inc.*, 115 S. Ct. 2371 (1995).

77. *See* DR 2-101(F). *See, e.g.,* Nassau County B.A. Comm. on Professional Ethics, Op. 93-29 (1993) (attorney may write to identified potential claimants in a class action); Nassau County B.A. Comm. on Professional Ethics, Op. 93-10 (1993) (attorney may write to potential clients who have placed "for sale" signs at their homes); Nassau County B.A. Comm. on Professional Ethics, Op. 93-1 (1993) (an attorney may write to clients who have been

charged with specific crimes and indicate he has represented people charged with similar crimes); Nassau County B.A. Comm. on Professional Ethics, Op. 90-7 (1990) (attorney may write to advertising agencies stating that he has been representing advertising agencies).

78. *See* DR 2-101(F). These materials may not advertise the fact of this filing. *See id.*

79. *See id.*

80. NYSBA Op. 659 (1994) (discussing inclusion of lawyer advertisement in automobile dealer's information packet).

81. *Id.*

82. *See* DR 2-102.

83. *See id.*

84. *See id.*

85. *See, e.g.,* ABA Comm. on Ethics and Professional Responsibility, Formal Op. 1515 (1985) (approving temporary booth for the preparation of simple wills at a carnival); Nassau County B.A. Comm. on Professional Ethics, Op. 93-29 (1993) (permitting clients to carry a banner on lawyer's behalf in a town parade).

86. *See* DR 2-104(E).

87. DR 2-104(C).

88. Even though seminars involve in-person communication, like solicitation, they appear to be accepted because they are communications to groups rather than individuals. *See* NYSBA Op. 508 (1979) (permitting seminars and targeted direct mail of invitations to seminars); ABA Comm. on Ethics and Professional Responsibility, Informal Op. 1179 (1971); ABA Comm., Informal Op. 804 (1965); *see generally* Nina Keilin, Note, *Client Outreach 101: Solicitation of Elderly Clients by Seminar Under the Model Rules of Professional Conduct*, 62 Fordham L. Rev. 1547 (1994).

89. DR 2-104(E).

90. NYSBA Op. 625 (1992).

91. *Id.*

92. *Id.*

93. *Id.*

94. NYSBA Op. 524 (1980).

95. DR 2-101(A). The Code generally describes marketing, including brochures and direct mail, other than prohibited solicitation as "advertising."

96. DR 2-101(K). The Appellate Division, Second Department, has rejected a challenge to this provision. *In re Anonymous*, 136 A.D.2d 344, 527 N.Y.S.2d 248 (2d Dep't 1988) (citing *Zauderer v. Office of Disciplinary Counsel of Supreme Court*, 471 U.S. 626, 650-51 (1985) (allowing reasonable requirements of disclosure of uncontroversial facts in order to prevent deception of consumers).

97. *See* DR 2-101(A). The New York State Bar Association Special Committee on Lawyer Advertising and Referral Service has proposed amending the Code of Professional Responsibility to define "false and misleading" in more detail. The committee suggests a new DR 2-101(B) providing as follows:

    2. False and misleading means any material representation, omission, act or practice which is likely to mislead persons acting reasonably in the circumstances, including, but not limited to, the following:
        a. A representation, omission, act or practice which refers to the prospective outcome of any legal matter, real or hypothetical, is false and misleading.
        b. A representation, omission, act or practice which implies influence with a court, court officer, governmental agency or government official is false and misleading.
        c. An advertisement is false and misleading if it contains any paid testimonial or endorsement without identifying the fact that payment has been made or, if the testimonial or endorsement is not made by an actual client, without identifying that fact.
        d. Except as stipulated in DR 2-103(D), that the attorney advertising intends that the attorney actually handling and/or trying the case will be someone other than the advertising attorney or a lawyer in his/her firm, without disclosing such fact.
        e. The terms "specialist," and "specializing in" are false and misleading except as provided in DR 2-105.

N.Y.S. Bar Association Special Comm. on Lawyer Advertising & Referral Service, Attorney Advertising Comm. Report 46-47 (Sept. 1995).

The committee also suggests a new EC 2-14 providing as follows:

EC 2-14 The following, if contained in advertising, may be considered to be of a false or misleading nature:

(a) Advertisements within a geographical area in which the advertising attorney has no staffed office, without such fact disclosed;

(b) A letter or other written advertising made to appear as a legal document;

(c) The inclusion of names, addresses and telephone numbers as required by DR 2-101(K) in a manner that is too small or too fast for an average viewer to receive the information in a meaningful fashion;

(d) The use of dollar signs, the terms "most cash" or "maximum dollars," or like terms which suggest the outcome of the legal matter;

(e) That the attorney advertising intends that the attorney actually handling and/or trying the case will be someone other than the advertising attorney or a lawyer in his/her firm, without disclosing such fact;

(f) Any representation that gives the inference that the advertising attorney will use greater effort than any other attorney;

(g) Use of an actor without disclosing such fact;

(h) Use of a dramatization without disclosing such fact. This list is not meant to be inclusive, but only illustrative.

Id. at 48-49.

98. *See, e.g.,* NYSBA Op. 624 (1991) (approving lawyer's mailing of truthful newspaper articles about the lawyer to potential clients provided that the articles did not create misleading expectations about the lawyer's services). For related information on the use of client testimonials, see page 193, "Testimonials."

99. *Zauderer v. Office of Disciplinary Counsel of Supreme Court*, 471 U.S. 626, 652 (1985).

100. *Id.*

101. *In re Zimmerman*, 79 A.D.2d 263, 438 N.Y.S.2d 400, 401-02 (4th Dep't), *appeal dismissed*, 53 N.Y.2d 937, 440 N.Y.S.2d 1029, 423 N.E.2d 416 (1981).

102. NYSBA Op. 640 (1992) (The titles Senior Paralegal, Staff Investigator, Office Manager, and Secretary are permissible. The title Paralegal Coordinator is not permissible because it is ambigu-

ous as to whether the person named is a paralegal. Similarly, the titles Legal Advocate or Family Law Advocate and the like are impermissible because they might lead Spanish speakers, who know that the word for lawyer in Spanish is *abogado*, to conclude that the named person is an attorney.)

103. DR 2-101(C)(1).

104. *See* NYSBA Op. 637 (1992) (a retired justice of the New York State Supreme Court should not hold himself out as a "Retired Justice of the Supreme Court," as that designation is misleading as to being the U.S. Supreme Court).

105. David Margolick, *At the Bar,* N.Y. Times, Apr. 9, 1993, p. B16.

106. *See* DR 2-101(C)(1).

107. *See* DR 2-102(D).

108. DR 2-101(C)(2).

109. DR 2-101(C)(3).

110. *Id.*

111. The lawyer is bound by this fee information (1) for a reasonable time but no less than 90 days if the publication has no fixed date for a succeeding issue, (2) until publication of the succeeding issue if the publication occurs once a month or less, and (3) for 30 days if the publication occurs more than once a month. The lawyer may charge more than an advertised fixed fee or fee schedule if the client agrees in writing to the different fee arrangement on the ground that the services were not those "referred to or implied in the advertisement or in the fee schedule." DR 2-101(G), (H).

112. DR 2-101(C)(4).

113. DR 2-105(A).

114. *See* notes 133-34, *infra,* and accompanying text.

115. *See, e.g., Zauderer v. Office of Disciplinary Counsel of Supreme Court*, 471 U.S. 626, 639-641 (1985) (discussing informing the public about the right to recover damages for personal injury).

116. Although governed in part by separate provisions, the rules for professional cards and letterheads are essentially the same as those for other communications. Professional cards may identify the lawyer "by name and as a lawyer, giving addresses, telephone numbers, the name of the law firm, and any information permitted under [DR

2-105]." DR 2-102(A)(1). They may also include "new or changed associations or addresses, change of firm name, or similar matters pertaining to the professional offices of a lawyer or law firm," "biographical data, the names of members of the firm and associates and the names and dates of predecessor firms," and the nature of the firm's practice as permitted under DR 2-105. DR 2-102(A)(2).

Letterhead may identify the lawyer by name and as a lawyer, and give addresses, telephone numbers, the name of the law firm, associations, and any information about the nature of the practice as permitted by DR 2-105. DR 2-102(A)(4). The letterhead of a firm may state "the names of members and associates, and names and dates relating to deceased and retired members," as well as the names and dates of predecessor firms. *Id.* A law firm that includes partners practicing as professional corporations must indicate this fact on its letterhead. Ass'n B. City N.Y. Comm. on Professional and Judicial Ethics, Formal Op. 80-40 (1980).

117. DR 2-102(A)(4). For other opinions elaborating on the appropriate use of the term "of counsel," see NYSBA Op. 262 (1972); Ass'n B. City N.Y. Comm. on Professional and Judicial Ethics, Op. 81-72 (1981); Ass'n B. City N.Y., Op. 81-109 (1981).

118. *See* DR 2-102(A)(4).

119. DR 2-101(B).

120. DR 2-101(A). We are not exactly certain what this phrase means. All marketing will cast some reflection on the bar. Perhaps it refers to a "negative" reflection; however, exactly what a "negative reflection" would be is unclear, and the restriction is problematic in light of the constitutional protections for commercial speech that is not false, deceptive, or misleading. *See* page 175 on the Constitution and commercial speech.

121. *Ibanez v. Florida Dep't of Business & Professional Regulation*, 114 S. Ct. 2084, 2088 (1994).

122. *Id.*

123. *Capoccia v. Comm. on Professional Standards*, No. 89-CV-866, 1990 U.S. Dist. LEXIS 17310, at *17 (N.D.N.Y. Dec. 20, 1990).

124. NYSBA Op. 661 n.1 (1994).

125. *Id.*

126. NYSBA Op. 614 (1990).

127. *Id. See also* Op. 661, note 124, *supra.*

128. *See* Op. 614, note 126, *supra.*

129. *See id.* The New York State Bar Association Committee on Professional Ethics opines that "[i]t would be unethical for the lawyer to compensate or give anything of value to the client to obtain the client's authorization for dramatized use of his or her testimonial." Op. 661, note 124, *supra* (relying on DR 2-103(B)).

130. Op. 614, note 126, *supra.*

131. *See Zauderer v. Office of Disciplinary Counsel of Supreme Court*, 471 U.S. 626 (1985) (attorney using illustration of Dalkon Shield intrauterine device in advertisement for personal injury clients).

132. NYSBA Op. 661, note 124, *supra.*

133. DR 2-105(B). *See also In re Peperone*, 201 A.D.2d 75, 615 N.Y.S.2d 212 (4th Dep't 1994) (entering order of censure for attorney using phrase "specializing in"). *But see* NYSBA Op. 363 (1974) (permitting use of term "specializes" in advertising to lawyers).

134. *See* DR 2-105(A); *Peperone*, 201 A.D.2d 75, 615 N.Y.S.2d 212.

135. Comm. on Professional Responsibility, *Advertising of Private Certification After Peel v. Illinois Attorney Registration and Disciplinary Commission*, 46 Rec. Ass'n B. City N.Y. 390, 391-92 (1991).

136. DR 2-102(B); Nassau County B.A. Comm. on Professional Ethics, Op. 90-16 (1990) (attorney may not use trade name "The Home Legal Clinic P.C.").

137. DR 2-102(B); NYSBA Op. 622 (1991).

138. DR 2-102(B).

139. *In re Von Wiegen*, 63 N.Y.2d 163, 481 N.Y.S.2d 40, 470 N.E.2d 838, 845 (1984), *cert. denied*, 472 U.S. 1007 (1985).

140. *Id.*

141. *See Taub v. Committee on Professional Standards for the Third Judicial District*, 200 A.D.2d 74, 612 N.Y.S.2d 272 (3d Dep't 1994) (vacating letters of education on procedural grounds).

142. *See Aponte v. Raychuk*, 172 A.D.2d 280, 568 N.Y.S.2d 735 (1st Dep't), *aff'd*, 78 N.Y.2d 992, 575 N.Y.S.2d 272, 580 N.E.2d 758

(1991). *See also* Dennis Hevesi, *Lawyers and Visa Services Charged in False Ads,* N.Y. Times, Sept. 28, 1991, p. 23 (detailing Department of Consumer Affairs charges against attorneys for misleading ads promising help with immigration lottery); Daniel Wise, *Immigration Lawyers'Ads Attract Attention*, N.Y.L.J. June 6, 1994, p. 1 (same).

143. *See, e.g., Baxter v. Ford Motor Co.* 12 P.2d 409 (Wash. 1932) (holding, among other things, that advertisers can be sued for breaches of promises made in advertising). The New York General Business Law also offers consumers a private right of action against anyone engaging in deceptive business practices or false advertising. *See* N.Y. Gen. Bus. Law §§ 349-350(e).

144. *See* Hazard, et al., note 6, *supra*, at 1099.

145. *See* the first part of this chapter, "The Ethics of Marketing Legal Services."

Bibliography

Abrams, Gary B. "Professional Telephone Strategies," (video), State Bar of Wisconsin, 1989.

Abrams, Gary B. "Professionalism in the Law Office," (video), State Bar of Wisconsin, 1987.

Beatty, M., and R. Martin. "A Blueprint for Avoiding Extinction," *Law Practice Management,* May-June 1994.

Beck, David J. "Advertising — Its Effect on Your Malpractice Exposure," *The Forum,* (American Bar Association Section of Tort and Insurance Practice), XVIII: 2, Winter 1983.

Bessen, Jim. "Riding the Marketing Information Wave," *Harvard Business Review,* September-October 1993.

"Beyond the Brochure," (program materials), *Section of Law Practice Management,* American Bar Association, 1988.

Blattberg, R.C., R. Glazer, and J. Little. *Marketing Information Revolution*, Boston: Harvard Business Press, 1993.

Bloom, P. N., "Effective Marketing for Professional Services," *Harvard Business Review,* September 1984.

Braun, Irwin, and Marilyn Braun. "Advertising versus Public Relations: You May Need Both," *Law Practice Management,* (American Bar Association Section of Law Practice Management) 14:4, May-June 1988.

Cobb, William C. "The Shift to the New Competitive Model and the Impact on Management Issues," *Law Practice Management,* May-June 1993.

"Finance and Marketing," *Computer Counsel*, 5:9, 1994.

Denney, Carole J., and Sandra Yost. "Keeping Happier Clients: How to Build and Improve Client Relations," American Bar Association, 1991.

Denney, Robert W., and Carol S. James. "Action Steps to Marketing Success: How to Implement Your Marketing Program," American Bar Association, 1991.

Denney, Robert W., Carol Jordan, and Sandra Yost. *Keeping Happier Clients: How to Build and Improve Client Relations.* Illinois: American Bar Association, 1991.

Derry, Michael. "Client Service Counts," *Law Practice Management,* October 1993.

Effective Marketing of Legal Services Through Advertising: A Practical Guide for Lawyers, Commission on Advertising, Chicago: American Bar Association, 1985.

Foonberg, Jay G. "A Five Minute Marketing Training Course," *Law Practice Management,* 6:3, April 1990.

Goldblatt, Michael L. *Organizing Successful Client Seminars*, Illinois: American Bar Association, 1990.

Goldblatt, Michael L. *Writing Your Law Firm Newsletter from Start to Finish*, Illinois: American Bar Association, 1987.

Gouillart, Francis J., and Frederick D. Sturdivant. "Spend a Day in the Life of Your Customers," *Harvard Business Review*, January-February 1994.

Hamel, Gary, and C. K. Prahalad. "Strategy as Stretch and Leverage," *Harvard Business Review,* March-April 1993.

Ilout, T. M., M. E. Porter, and E. Rudden. "How Global Companies Win Out," *Harvard Business Review*, September 1982.

Johansson, Nonaka I. "Marketing Research the Japanese Way," *Harvard Business Review,* May 1987.

Kosnik, T. J., "Corporate Positioning: How to Assess — and Build — A Company's Reputation," *Harvard Business Review*, December 1989.

Krocheski, J., and G. Malone. "Opening the Lines of Communication with Clients," *Law Practice Management,* 6:28, September 1994.

Kunzke, Katja. "Lawyer Advertising: Does It Work," *Membernet* (American Bar Association Young Lawyers Division Membership Support Network), October 1989.

LaBorde, Genie Z. Influencing with Integrity, Syntony Publishing, 1983.

Lane, Robert E. *The Market Experience*, Cambridge: Cambridge University Press, 1991.

Levitt, T. *Levitt on Marketing*, Boston: Harvard Business Press, 1990.

Levitt, Theodore. "The Gray Area; The Poetry of Becoming," *Harvard Business Review*, March-April 1993.

Lovelock, Carlson L. "New Gold Mines and Minefields in Market Research," *Harvard Business Review,* December 1984.

Manassero, William J. "Developing a Small Firm Strategic Practice Marketing Plan," *Law Practice Management,* 13:8 November-December 1987.

Maxwell, Kimera K., and Roger W. Reinsch. "A Lawyer's Guide to Public Relations: The Art of Promoting Your Practice," *Professional Education System*, (State Law Library Young Lawyers Division Collection), Wisconsin, 1989.

Mintzberg, Henry. "The Rise and Fall of Strategic Planning," *Harvard Business Review,* 72:107, January-February 1994.

Montgomery C. A., and M. E. Porter. *Strategy: Seeking and Securing Competitive Advantage,* Boston: Harvard Business Press, 1991.

Munneke, G. "Law Firm Reconstructing: The Big Picture," *Law Practice Management*, April 1993.

New York State Bar Association Client Relations Kit, "One Client at a Time."

O'Steen, Van. "Advertising as a Marketing Tool," *Law Practice Management,* February 1986.

Porter, M. E. "How Competitive Forces Shape Strategy," *Harvard Business Review*, March 1979.

Porter, M. E. and V. E. Millar. "How Information Gives You Competitive Advantage," *Harvard Business Review,* July 1985.

Porter, M. E. *Porter on Competition and Strategy*, Boston: Harvard Business Press, 1990.

Practice Development for Women Lawyers (Program Materials), Mass: Continuing Legal Education, Inc., 1994

Raridon, Susan. *Basic Writing for Your Law Firm Brochure,* Illinois: American Bar Association, 1987.

Raridon, Susan. "Satisfied Clients Bring in New Clients," *Law Practice Management,* 13:1, January-February 1987.

Reynolds, Ward W. "The Case Against Lawyer Advertising," *ABA Journal,* January 1989.

RoAne, Susan. "How to Work a Room," Audio Renaissance Tapes, Inc., 1991.

Rocheleau, Anne. "Making Your Practice More Elder Friendly," *Law Practice Management,* May-June 1993.

Secrets of Effective Public Speaking, (video), American Bar Association, 1990.

Slywotzky, Adrian J., and Benson P. Shapiro. "Leveraging to Beat the Odds: The New Marketing Mind-Set," *Harvard Business Review*, September-October 1993.

Tolman, Jeff. "Choose Me: A Little Self-Promotion Can Be Classy and Still Go a Long Way," *The Compleat Lawyer* (American Bar Association Section of General Practice) 6:3, Summer 1989.

Women Rainmakers (video), American Bar Association.

Zibron, Nancy A. "Starting a Speakers Bureau," *Law Practice Management,* 15:8, November 1989.

Christine S. Filip

Chris Filip is an attorney and president of The Success Group in Manhattan. Her company assists firms in developing unique marketing strategies that create wealth. Chris is an expert at leveraging persuasion skills, both face-to-face and in the print and broadcast media, so that rainmaking results.

Chris began her professional career with IBM in 1973, and made the 100% Club for sales excellence in her rookie year. Chris spent nine years with Savin and left the company as the general manager of the New York office. She founded Success Consulting in 1988 to bring the power of marketing to professionals.

In addition to her practice, Chris is a sought-after speaker on rainmaking and business development. She teaches advanced seminars on marketing and negotiations skills at New York University. She is the monthly marketing columnist for *New Jersey Lawyer*, and her column is reprinted in legal and business publications across the United States. Her articles have appeared in the *Massachusetts Lawyers Weekly, New York Law Journal, American Management Association Business Reports, Brooklyn Barrister*, and *Sales and Marketing Management Magazine*, among others.

She is a member of the Massachusetts Bar and the commercial panel of the American Arbitration Association. She holds a B.A., an M.Ed., and a Juris Doctor.